FEEDLOTS, RANCHES, AND ROPIN

FEEDLOTS, RANCHES, AND ROPIN

EL JEFE

authorHOUSE®

AuthorHouse™
1663 Liberty Drive
Bloomington, IN 47403
www.authorhouse.com
Phone: 1-800-839-8640

Published by AuthorHouse   11/20/2012

ISBN: 978-1-4772-9320-1 (sc)
ISBN: 978-1-4772-9319-5 (e)

Library of Congress Control Number: 2012921963

Contents

Ranches

Ropin

In the preparation of this book, there are a few people to thank:

The Verde Girls
Annette * Michelle * Debbie
Thanks for your support

My life-long friend, John, whose moral support is greatly appreciated

The hard work and patience of Stephanie, who did the proof-reading and corrections, and liaison work.

And, lastly, Mrs. Jefe, who raised three children in a world of drugs, alcohol, and still turned out quality people. All the while tolerating the whims of a heavily addicted cowpuncher.

Feedlots

Black Eye

Years ago, when I was workin at a now defunct feedlot, there was a guy there who was always in dutch with his wife. He was great; she was great; but one beer together and it was war!! One day, he came to work with a black eye. What happened, we all asked. She gave it to me when she was doin the laundry. Why, we ask. Yesterday, when we was markin those steers with that red markin chalk, I got some on my hands then it rubbed off on my underwear when I went pee. She saw the red chalk and thought it was lipstick, then she gave me the eye!!!

Which Horse was Most Efficient

Years ago, when I was a button, I was workin for a feed yard that was run by a sure nuff real deal cowboy/cowman. We saddled up at 3:30, summer or winter. I was catchin my pony one mornin and Sam was showin the new man his horses by the light of a single danglin light bulb. This cat had a pair of Gene Autry bat-wing chaps, a pair of Buffalo Bill gauntlets, and a wire brim JC Penny felt hat. I heard Sam groan as the guy asked which horse was the most efficient!!!!

Jack the Coffee Thief

Years ago, when I was the cow boss at a now defunct feed yard, there was a little guy who worked there who reminded me of a yappin little lap dog that peed on everything. We also had a gal pen rider who was damn good and tough. We all brought our coffee in thermoses for a break at mid-mornin. The gal would always bring a flovoured coffee, and Jack would sneak in and drink it when she wasn't lookin. One day, when she came to work, she put her thermos in the usual place and warned us all not to touch it. Later that mornin, we saw Jack sneak into the saddle room and sample the coffee. Didn't see him no more for three days. She had doctored it with Ex-Lax and Croton Oil!!!

Cow Bell for the New Bride

Years ago, when I was a button, I was workin for an outfit that had a head cowboy who got married. He had been quite a ladies man, so a friend of mine and I got into their house before they came home from the wedding; to the bed springs we hung a cow bell. The new bride didn't come out of the house for a week and the groom wouldn't speak to any of us for two days!!!

Barry Baby Brashears

Here's one for you Verde Valley folks that know Barry "Baby" Brashears. Years ago, he and another puncher were workin for me in a feedyard. The rule was: no ropin for fun. The boss was death on it. As a matter of fact, he had put the word out that the next one he caught was history. Barry, Kim, and me were in a pen ropin on a Saturday evening when the boss called on the two-way wantin me in the office. I loped up there and tied my horse outside. When we finished what we had to do, the boss asked me to take his blazer and gas it up. I could see the boys ropin, so I idled down close and then gunned the engine and spun tires all the way to them. Ropes flew outta the pen every which way. I was smilin as I cruised by!!! Boys weren't happy!!!

Old Hoot

Old Hoot was a hell of an old cowboy, but as time overtook him he became an alcoholic with no bounds. We tolerated him as long as he was halfway sober, but more than half the time, we sent him home. One mornin, shipping fat cattle, it was a hour before daylight, but we had a big yeller moon. Four of us went into the pen to drive the steers to the gate and into the alley, but only three of us went out the gate. We turned back to see Hoot drivin his own shadow down the fence, cussin it for not goin out the gate!!! Hoot went home that day.

Young and Reckless

When I was young and reckless, I was workin at a now defunct feedlot that had a poor attitude toward cowboys. We were shippin fat cattle one mornin in the rain. I was in the lead in the dark with a poncho over my head in a drivin rain. Ole Chickin, the long-legged horse I was ridin, pulled the plug in the middle of about two feet of mud and manure. The first jump, my knees were in the seat of my saddle. Ole Chick bucked on down the alley, but as I struggled to my feet, he ran over me again goin the other way. As I got up, he came over me again. This happened four or five times until that bunch of idiots behind me figured out there was a gate shut in front of me and they caught the horse!!

Last Feedlot

Years ago when I was a button, I went to work at the last feedlot in Phoenix. It was bordered by 48th street on the west, Washington on the north, with the Salt River on the south. There were two old punchers who had been there since Noah unloaded the boat. Buster was a big man and kinda quiet, Homer Lee was about five feet tall and could talk a blue streak. The sensitive noses in the neighborhood complained about the smell, so the owners had put in a mister system along 48th that put out a perfume. The first mornin it was workin, we all were ridin along the line. Homer went to wavin his hand in front of his face, whwh ew, my wife will think I smell like a whorehouse. Without lookin up, Buster mumbled: how would your wife know what a whorehouse smelled like? The fight was on!!!!

No Pencil

Years ago, I went to work for a large feedlot with 60 thousand head as a pen rider. After I was there a couple weeks, the super drove up in his pickup. "GO DOWN TO PEN SO AND SO AND GIVE ME A HEAD COUNT, AND WRITE IT DOWN." I told the old man I had no pencil but I could write it down on my Copenhagen can if I had a pencil. He opened the glove box and pulled out a new box of Eagle pencils. Handing me one, he told me to cut off what I needed and give him the rest back!!! I carried that stub of pencil all the time I worked there, in my hatband!!

Breezy

Breezy had a temper, and it showed up one cold January mornin. We had stopped at the scale house and got a cup of Joe to warm up a bit. The super made a wiseass remark about us not bein good enough to be inside, so we took our cups of coffee with us and left. Breezy's horse was a little blue roan called Tiger who, the more you fussed with, jigged and acted up. The alley was knee-deep in mud and muck. We were easin along, tryin not to spatter each other, when Tiger started cuttin up. Breezy was already mad from what the super said, so he just poured that cup of hot coffee down ole Tiger's ear!!!! So much for stayin clean!!!

Purple Continental

In the 70s and 80s, it was good economic practice for people with lots of money to invest in feedlot cattle. A black comedian was a big plunger as long as the cattle were black. With the rage on in Angus cattle, I'd say he knew somethin. Mike and I were workin at a now defunct feedlot when on a Saturday mornin before daylight, we could hear a radio playin down in the pens. As it got light, we ambled down into the yard and in a pen of fat cattle was a purple Continental stuck in a mud hole, the doors were open, fat steers rubbin on the car, brushin up against it and knockin dents into it. As we got closer, we could see whiskey bottles scattered around and feet back inside the car's front and back seats. A little closer and we realized it was a couple of popular movie stars. I won't use their names because one is still with us. It turned out they were lookin for their cattle. We got a tractor to pull the car to dry land and the yard boss took those two cattle barons to the airport, so ends that episode, never to return those two!!

Anson

Anson was a big ole kid, kinda slow, but willing as all get out. He liked to rope and his summer job at the feedlot fit right in. He had a big ole platter-footed horse that couldn't run fast enough to scatter his own droppings with a rake tied in his tail!!! We were practicing one afternoon after work when Anson decided to help the chute help move a steer up into the roping chute. But instead of getting off his horse, he hung his rope with a loop built over the saddle horn and leaned over the side to push the steer. Just as he was leaning off the side of his horse, the header called for the steer! Three horses left in pursuit of the steer, the header, the heeler, and ole platter-foot, with Anson's foot hung in that big loop!!! Anson's fanny was plowing a furrow down the arena you could plant corn in!! When we got ole platter-foot stopped, Anson got up, kicked the horse in the butt and said, "why can't you run that fast when I'm on your back!!"

I Buy Ya Beer and Pay Ya to Drink it

When I was the YARD BOSS AT THE SPUR FEEDLOT IN SAN TAN, Arizona, we had a real wet winter goin on. It had rained so much the corrals were knee deep in mud and slop. We had a full house with more cattle comin in every night. Many times, the cattle that came in stood in an alley all night until we emptied a corral of fat cattle the next mornin. For six weeks, we were at a long trot from before daylight to after dark and sometimes later. The superintendent was a young man, fresh married and out of college. Unlike most, he was a great guy in that position and handled pressure like a pro. We had hired a couple day labors to help with the increasing load. Sick cattle, fat cattle to sort, thousands to process and brand. One of the few sunshiny days, the super came by where I was sortin fats. I'm gonna buy us a case of beer and tonight, I didn't care what or what needs doin, everyone be at the saddle house at five, were gonna have a beer. I spread the word and everyone perked up a little!

Sure enough, at 5 o'clock, Jr. drove up with a case of beer. He even passed it out to everyone and, with a smile, told us all what a great job we were doin and thanked us all for our devotion to duty. The regular crew was salaried, but the two day men were on by the hour. After the second round, Jr. looked at the day men. "Did you clock out?" he asked. They smiled and shook their heads. Jr. dropped his beer and ran into the saddle room where we heard the clock bang twice. As he came out he said, "damn, i buy ya beer and pay ya to drink it!!!"

It was a good time. Little did we know, a month later Jr. and his wife would be dead in a plane wreak while on a Christmas vacation and honeymoon. We sure missed him, a great guy.

A Bank and a Steer

Well, here is a cowboy story that was requested by the blonde bomber. Years ago, at the Phoenix stockyards, a bank was built to accommodate the cattle feeders and livestock industry in general. It sat on the corner of 48th and Washington in a big ole lot that had been cattle pens. It was paved and open to the world. This was in the days before shatterproof glass, and this bank had giant plate glass windows along the front. Well as in most cattle situations, there were cattle crawling out of the feedlot and wandering around the neighborhood. We very seldom had cattle go as far as the bank and stockyard's restaurant or the set of office buildings that made up the cattleman's complex. The bank manager was a self-righteous S.O.B. that thought of us workin, shit-kickin punchers as less than human. One day, just before noon, the feed truck informed us that a steer was wandering around the complex and could we get him before that banker called the boss. We struck a trot up that way; it wasn't far. Well, this particular steer was a chronic offender about gettin out and visiting the neighborhood. Those cattle usually got a dose of nylon rope injected with a strong right arm on a big stout horse. This particular steer had already been given this treatment a time or two, so when he saw us comin decided to make himself scarce! When he trotted past the front of the bank he saw his own reflection in that big plate glass window and just naturally thought he should hide with that steer! He jumped through that window right into the bank lobby!! When we got there, the tellers were up on the counter and that pompous banker was pleading for someone to come here and bring someone with them!!! I slipped in a foot, roped ole steer and gave the rope to a man outside who led him out. You know, there wasn't a speck of cow shit in that bank!

Smokey

When I worked at Arizona Land and Cattle, they had cattle interests all over Arizona, Colorado, and New Mexico. One of their outfits was an alfalfa pasture and growing yard in Florence, Arizona. The man taking care of it quit and there was no one there to look after things. It was about 20 miles from where I was, so I was elected to drive down and look after the cattle until a new man was hired.

The alfalfa fields were fenced in electric fencing so you needed to be there every day. I didn't need to take a horse, Smokey had left a good string there, and as how he was renown for making good horses, I knew I would be mounted well.

The first day I caught a good bay to ride. Man, he was nice, traveled good, was gentle and when I tried out ropin a pinkeye steer you couldn't have ask for a better mount. As I was ridin in that afternoon, a little piece of bailing wire flipped out of the weeds and ole bay stampeded! He ran about 100 yards before I got him stopped. As time went on, I found that every horse there would do that if a wire or string brushed up against their leg, yet they were all good to shoe and gentle to work around.

A few years later, I ran into a feller who worked for Smokey there and I asked what caused those good horses to act so. He said when Smokey wanted to test the electric fence, he was always forgetting the tester so he would just back his horse into it to see if it was hot!!!

One Steer Standing

Years ago, when I worked for the new Toverea feed yard in Maricopa, we were rollin. The Swift packing plant in Tolleson had opened up and was killin cattle at an amazin rate for that day and time. The trucking industry in Arizona wasn't prepared for the onslaught, so every conceivable kind of truck was pressed into service. Most were truck and pull trailers, single deck with ply board sides held together with cable!! You talk about scary, 40 head of fat cattle goin down the road weavin back and forth, spooky!

One mornin, I was loadin one of 15 or 20 trucks to go to Tolleson. Two trucks had already left loaded. The scale house door flew open and the boss ran out, jumped in his truck, spun around, and headed down the road like his tail was on fire!! Behind him, the other three cowboys jumped on their horses and left in a lope, yellin at me to come when I got done. I ask, "where?" They pointed to where the road crossed the train tracks. I looked that way and could see one steer standing on a trailer with no side boards; the truck was nowhere in sight. At the time there, was no crossin arms on the track, so a sleepy-headed driver pulled in front of a train. The train hit where the truck and trailer coupled. The truck was still movin and only lost the boards on the tail end. The shock of the collision had shattered the boards on the trailer all the cattle but one being killed. When I got there that steer was still on the naked trailer and the driver was froze to the wheel!!

Last Train Load

In the early 70s, I was privileged to be working for a feed yard who probably took delivery on the last trainload of cattle to be delivered in that manner. When they built this feed yard, they installed a rail siding. Which, to my knowledge, was used just this once.

These cattle came directly out of Mexico, also an unheard of thing for that day and time. As I remember, there were 38 forty-foot cars with between 60 and 40 head to each car. The bulls were tied in the corners of each car with inch cotton rope, which was the custom of the day. Once again, being the youngest (and dumbest), it fell to me when a car was spotted at the chute, I would slide the door open, climb the inside wall, and walk around the inside of the wall and push the cattle out. Anything tied, I then untied and got them out. Now, a Mexican bull, tied with his head in the corner for 48 hours is not a happy camper!! There isn't near as much room in one of those cars as one would think!! Before we were finished, the legs of my Wranglers were shredded. Sometimes the bulls didn't want to leave the car. So who do you think was elected to tease the animal into charging down the chute? Yup, old dumb shit!! We finished unloading in the dark, no lights, and it was a full mile to the scales. Everyone's horses were pooped, not to mention us.

This trainload of cattle had been put together in Mexico in small bunches, so there was every kind of animal mixed in, from old work oxen with holes bored through their horns for driving lines down to a six month old calves. We sorted for days and then branded them through the squeeze chute for another week. I could be wrong, but I believe this was the one and only trainload of cattle unloaded there, and possibly the last one in Arizona.

T&C Cattle Co

When I got out of high school and was goin to college part-time, I worked for the Tovrea feedlots under the name T&C Cattle Co. When I learned the boss was leavin, I decided I didn't want to stay either. I had a little socked away: a new pickup and a single-horse trailer with a fair kinda head horse. After takin the summer off, I figured I needed a job. Another feedlot came callin on a Sunday mornin. I went to work on Monday. In those days, everything I owned fit in the camper on the pickup and the saddle compartment of that trailer, so the move was easy. For six years at Tovreas, every animal that was sick was roped and doctored. If he weighed 1400 or 200, he got roped! No squeeze chute doctorin there, but when ropin the cattle, they weren't rodeoed either. I have helped doctor 25 head of calves out of 100 in a corral, roped everyone and NEVER got an animal out of a walk. We were just a level above most other feedlots. At the new feedlot, cowboys weren't allowed to use a rope. Most didn't even carry one. My second day there, we were comin up a feed alley when we found a big fat steer upside-down in the feed bunk. In his pickup, there was the super. I was the only cowboy there with a rope. The super pointed to me and told me to pull that steer out. No, I told him. When you hired me, you told me I would get fired for taken that rope down. Pull the steer out and I'll never say a word to you!! I pulled the steer out and over the next three years I worked there, I could rope whatever NEEDED roping and never a word said. But, during that three years, he fired three or four men just for swinging a rope while driving cattle down an alley!!!

Pancho

PANCHO was a Mexican cowboy at Hughes and Ganz feed yard. He had been there since it was built, before actually, as he was irrigating the land when the feedlot was built. He was little thick in the middle, didn't speak very plain English, rode a Montgomery ward saddle, and used a Jap-made bit on all his horses, but make no mistake, he was all cowboy. One of his horses was a big, feather-legged ole pony that was black, bald-faced, and stockin-legged. Maybe somewhere his ancester pulled a plow, but that ole pony was a cow horse, especially when Pancho rode him.

11

Now that ole pony was gentle, but he would tolerate no foolishness. One mornin, while it was still dark and Pancho was sippin coffee in the scale house, three of us saddled ole baldy with the saddle on backwards!! It was a fight and it took all three of us to do it. When Pancho saw this, he grinned and shook his head, but that was all. One of the guys, who was the ringleader in this little prank, was a pickup driver boss. The next day, the keys to his pickup were gone we searched high and low, but no keys. He got a new ignition set for the truck. In the scale house was a mounted steer head with a big set of horns. One day, while sittin there with a cup of coffee, I happened to look up at that head. A set of keys hung from one horn. Wonder how that happened? Pancho only smiled!!

Working Cattle in the Glades

Not long ago, I commented in a post about an outfit I worked for having a ranch in Florida and the cattle comin out of the trucks with gaters snappin at their heels. Here is the story:

When I had just went to work for AZL, they had bought a 3000 head ranch in Florida. Why they felt they needed the cattle in Arizona, I don't know, but as the cracker cowboys put a load together, they put wheels under them and smoke over them and sent them swamp angels west. By the time they hit the ground in Queen Creek, Arizona, they were for sure ringy. A lot of those cattle hadn't been gathered in years and they were sure upset to lose their homes in the palmetto forests. Very few would drink out of a trough or were safe to walk through a foot, as the water trough washer found out.

These cattle were all over 800 pounds on arrival, after a 2000 mile trip, so it took them a few days to recover, then there was hell amongst the yearlins. A feed truck would drive by and they all crashed into the fences at the back side of the corrals. When a pen rider went into the pen he had to pay attention to where he was at all times. If somethin startled them suckers you could get run over big time. They didn't look where they were goin when they ran.

After about six months, the company higher ups decided it must be the poor help in Florida, what with poppin them whips and all that made them cattle like that. So, they hired a bunch of sure enough Arizona cowpunchers, and sent a manager from Queen Creek there to show them crackers how to do IT. Well, the manager stayed, but them Arizona punchers came home in six weeks. Them people are nuts, they told me. It wasn't people made them cattle crazy, it was the gaters, the skeeters and heel flies, and worst of all, the damn hurricanes.

Old Scooter

Old Scooter was a plain ole sorrel pony that had spent his whole life in the stockyards in Phoenix workin for the Tovera family. He was sure-footed, stout on a rope, and could cut a cow with the best of them. He had one problem: he didn't like needles, not one bit. I've seen unsuspecting fellows walk into his stall with a needle in hand and escape with their lives!! I know, I was one! When it came time to give Scooter a shot, you went into the stall with a bridle, then blindfolded him, hobbled him, twisted an ear, and you MIGHT give him the shot!! But, with that he was a great cow pony. And, in a pinch, you could haul him to a ropin and be competitive!!

Clayton was the cattle buyer for Tovera, and very seldom got horseback, but would on occasion. It had rained steady for a week. The pens were ankle deep in soup, and slick as ice under the soup. We all had been down at least once as it was just scary as hell in those pens. Those old pens didn't have alleys to sort in, so three men would hold the cattle at one end of a corral while the boss would cut the fats out past you. Then when he had enough, we would put the cuts in the feed alley and drive them to the scales.

When Clayton came to sort, he always borrowed ole Scooter. In the trunk of the Cadillac he drove, he carried a handmade Van Core saddle, two Navajo blankets, and a salinas-ported Garcia bit on a filigreed headstall. Ole Scooter looked like a showboat with all that hoss jewelry. We were sortin some fats one day after the rain let up. Clayton, for all his loud talk, fancy outfit, and cigar smokin, was a top hand. We had sorted 20 head or so, all of us puckered up with our saddle seats halfway up our rectums, when Clayton started a big ole crossbred steer. No matter what we did, we couldn't get out of the way enough for Clayton to put that steer outta the herd. After the third or fourth dash across the pen, ole Scooter had enough. He put his shoulder into that steer, bit him in the neck, and they ran along together to the feed bunk with Clayton's face as white as a bed sheet. When they got to the feed bunk, Scooter jumped up on the concrete apron and slid with all four feet locked up!! The steer went down, then turned and trotted to the cuts. Clayton had bit his cigar in two and was froze to the saddle horn like death on a grim cowpuncher. Under his breath we heard him say, "You damned old scrub... cow when I tell ya to cow"!!

Kosher Buyer

The cattle market was in the tank. I know, so what's new? But this was the early 70s and AZL was trying to get rid of too many cattle that cost too much and were eating their heads off and the packers didn't want 'em at any price. I had sorted this one set of Angus steers so many times my wife was telling me in the mornins if I called her by in my sleep one more time, I would get real acquainted with the couch!! We had gotten down to the last four truckloads of steers in this one particular lot. There wasn't a nickel's worth of difference in any of them. They were too light, still eating more than they could gain, and the packer buyers still looked the other way when they drove by. I had, at the request of the fat seller, re-sorted for the third or fourth time this bunch of losers before we went to lunch. When I came back an hour later, the seller was waiting at the saddle house. He had showed that bunch of over-fed midgets to a potential kosher buyer during lunch and he said he would take one certain pen if I would re-sort and shape them up!! I about fell over. I had done everything but paint 'em pink, I told the seller. He agreed, but ask couldn't I do SOMETHING? I told him to give me an hour to come up with somethin. When he was outta sight, I saddled my horse and went to the two pens these cattle lived in. I looked at the cattle in the pen the kosher buyer wanted and then at the other pen. Same cattle, I could find no difference. So in desperation, I switched pens with the cattle. Three that afternoon, the seller came around with a big smile on his face. I don't know what you did, but he liked it so much he bought the fronts and the tailender at two dollars back!!! But they were the same cattle, I said!! The seller said the buyer thought no one coulda sorted them any better! From then on, I had to live up to that stunt as the best fat cattle sorter in Arizona!!! Out of the frying pan, into the fire!!!

Bone-Headed Stunt

While at AZL, we turned lots of steers out on ranches the company owned. Usually, we would turn them out in October and hope for winter rain to liven the desert up. Problem was, if it didn't rain, those cattle would starve if you didn't get them off. Usually, they were light-weight steers from Mexico. Many times, we sent cattle out to pasture and, in 60 days, got them back weighing less than they did when we shipped them out.

The ranch super, who was in charge of all the Arizona ranches, sometimes pulled some bone-headed stunts. The monsoons had filled the dirt tanks on the lower deserts and made a few Mesquite beans, but this one fall, it was still dry and not a lot of feed out there. We had four thousand little Mexican steers shaped up and ready to go the moment the rains hit. Sure enough, in mid-October, it rained four days straight. On the fifth day, we loaded the trucks and put wheels under the little guys and sent them to the desert. It was a BIG gamble, but the ranch super was a big plunger when he had someone else's checkbook! Sure enough, it didn't rain another drop. The green sprouted and dried back to a dusty, brown scrub. The ranch manager called me and hollered for help. He didn't have enough help to gather and ship that four thousand little steers. He said the super was makin him hold them hoping for rain, but he was afraid they would be too weak to survive a cold rain. Damned if you do, damned if you don't. I sent four of my best men to that dust bowl ranch to help gather and ship the steers. It was twelve miles of dirt road into the headquarters across an adobe flat that would bog a saddle blanket, if wet, and choke you to death in the dust, when dry. The second day of December, it started rainin. The crew was stuck there. It rained for a week, then they got three days of sunshine, but the ground was too wet to drive out. On the fourth day, the rain came back for two more days. Instead of shippin, those boys were doctoring and pullin the weak steers out of mud holes. It was almost two weeks before I got my crew back. And those little steers didn't get back until May, but they were a lot bigger than when they went. But I swore I would never send my cowboys out like that again, 'cause the workload at home was a double up on those left there.

Homer

Homer had been at the Tovera stockyards his whole life. The only other job he had was in the army in WWII. When I got there, he was a few weeks from retirement. He was a hoot! His favorite mount was an old grey horse, called Turdy, and every other horse he rode was Turdy, Jr. His horses were so fat, his legs stuck straight out from the sides of his saddle. He wasn't much over five foot tall. He wore the biggest brim hat he could find and chewed Day's Work plug tobacco. When he spit, he spit upwards and it hit the brim of his hat and then would dribble down into the wind to be blown back into his face.

Year round, summer or winter, he wore a Levi jacked, buttoned at the throat with the rest unbuttoned. When it was cold and he complained about it, someone suggested he button the rest of the buttons on the jacket. He simply said it wouldn't do no good no how!! Same response in the summer when he complained about the heat and someone suggested he take the jacket off.

For all of his silliness, Homer was a damned good cowboy. It was said he knew when a steer was gonna get sick before the steer did. He roped good, but always with a tied rope. Every month he got a new rope. The company had an account at the local livestock supply outfit and we were allowed a new rope once a month. Homer made sure he got his on the first of every month. His old rope was just barely broke in. We found out later he traded the old one at a bar for whiskey.

One day, we were about to doctor a big, fat steer that had an abscess on his ribs. We circled the steer around the pen a couple times tryin to get a clean throw at him. He weighed about 1400 pounds and we all knew whoever caught the head had to have a good lick and keep his horse on its feet in the slick pens. Presently, the steer came trotin by Homer and old Turdy. Homer had a monster loop swingin and just cast it out in front of old steer. He caught him. The steer behind and alongside when those two hit the end of the rope, old Turdy did a hand stand in front, his tail popped up behind, and Homer was launched like a rocket. He landed astraddle of cable fence and fell into a water trough with his mouth open and no sound comin out. Someone got Turdy loose and the rest of us got Homer out of the water trough. All he said when he looked around was that the steer didn't need no attention!!!

Rabies!!!

It had been a wet winter and the feedlot at San Tan was full and knee-deep in mud. Cattle were comin and goin daily as we processed and straightened out the health on untold numbers of cattle comin from every direction of the compass. When the southwestern Arizona deserts get rain, there isn't enough cattle to eat all the grass. Joe and I were takin care of a couple of long alleys of grass cattle, prob'ly five thousand head. We were short-handed, short-tempered, and just plain tired. The boss and his wife had been killed in a plane wreck, and all the knowledge on all these cattle had been locked in his head. Joe and I had a good idea about a lot of them just from memory, but, it turns out, nobody knew for sure. If some cat off the street had walked in and claimed he owned five hundred head, there was no way to prove it one way or another.

Everyday someone we didn't know called about his cattle and when could they go to grass. The girl in the office was plumb stumped. A lot of those guys were partners in bunches of cattle, and the irons were leased from the company. Without some kind of paperwork, there wasn't hardly any way to tell whose was what. We began by tearin the deceased boss's pickup apart. The keys had been in his pocket when he died and no one had a clue where they went. After a couple hours, we came up with a small tally book. In it were some transactions that he had meant to record at a later date and hadn't gotten around to. By using this book, we began to piece together owners and cattle. One particular string had come out of Mexico and was a partnership deal with a particularly obnoxious fellow and the company. This partner was an Okie car dealer and he called daily, being a nuisance. He wanted those cattle on grass, and NOW!! I had a couple of heated discussions with this cat and, almost daily, he had the office girl crying. A new boss was comin, but it would be a month before he got there. We had to hold it together the best we could.

One afternoon, as Joe and I were checkin these Mexican-Okie partnership cattle, we noticed a brown steer runnin like crazy from one end of the pen to the back, and back again. This steer was bawlin like a mad man, runnin into other cattle and bouncin off the fences. There was no way to cut this steer out of the pen, so as he came by, Joe roped him around the neck and I roped one hind foot. Keeping the steer between us, we see sawed him down to the hospital pen. We were able to keep this loco from getting next to our horses or us and, when we had him in the crowding pen at the hospital, we threw our ropes in with him. I struck a lope to the office and called the state vet. We knew it was rabies!! The vet advised us to keep an eye on that steer and make no contact with him. while in the office the Okie car dealer called with his daily whine. I told him to stop calling, his cattle were quarantined for rabies and whoever he bought them from was responsible. That shut him up. I told him I would call and advise him when the state vet got through. The next day, the vet showed and that damned steer was as normal as you could get, no symptoms at all. The vet drew some blood and said he would call back. He didn't think he had rabies, but couldn't tell us what was wrong. The next day, the vet called and still had no answers, but the steer was still acting normal, so we put him in a pen with other cattle. After two weeks, that steer was the fattest one in the pen, no rabies. I ordered trucks and shipped the cattle in that group to grass, then I called Mr. Okie car dealer told him they were gone. I thought that would make him happy. Nope. I got my butt chewed for lettin that steer get rabies!!! Can't win!!

Ropin the Bulls

While at AZL, I was able to work with some good cowboys and ropers. One was my good friend Joe. He was a natural roper, horseman, and prankster!! He came from a long line of cowboys and rodeo hands, his own dad winning the Prescott rodeo a number of times.

At any feedlot, there is always a few bull calves that escape the knife due to sickness, lameness, and any number of other reasons. And, if things are real busy, might be forgotten about for a month or two. In that amount of time they get BIG!! At AZL, they had a crew of fellows we called the vets. They weren't really veterinarians, but they drove around in pickups, doctored the sick cattle in each alley when the cowboys found them, and put them in a hospital pen with a squeeze chute for that purpose. Once in a while, when things slowed down, they would recruit a couple of us with itchy arms and ropes and we would rope the missed bulls and stretch them out while the vets conducted brain surgery on those bulls.

This one day, they got Joe and me to help put down a half dozen of these bulls. The first bull trotted by and Joe flipped an overhand loop at the bull, ropin him around the neck with the loop figure-eighting the front feet. When the slack came tight, the bull laid down on his side with both front feet pulled up under his jaw. All I had to do was trot up and drop my loop over the hind feet. When stretched out the bull couldn't choke because his front feet acted like a block, keeping the rope from choking him. No fuss, no muss. When the vet was through, he laughed and said: too bad Joe couldn't do that every time!! Joe said he could, and would, for a case of beer!! The vet called the bet!!

After work that night, Joe and I had a cold beer at those boys' expense!! And ya know, Joe never let them forget it either!!

Eatin is Just a Habit

My old friend Clayton had taken over the Arlington feedlot and was needin some cowboys. I was outta work and had two kids, a wife, and a third kid on the way, and all there was between us and starvation was the winnins from a jackass ropin. We moved to Arlington. It was a heck of a deal. We were given a four bedroom frame house that a bachelor cowboy was campin in, AND I mean campin!! The bachelor was gonna leave in a month or so and just needed a bed room and a chance to eat three squares, or so we were told. After a half day of scoopin out the trash and whatever, we moved in and settled somewhat. I went to work the next mornin along with the bachelor and three other hands, one of whom was my old friend Pete. He had been there a few months longer than me and had been recruited by Clayton, same as me.

Pete and I kinda paired up and rode together, as we had worked together for six years at Toveras. Once in a while, the bachelor would ride with us, but mostly he was the floater fillin in on someone's day off. When the first day came to an end and we all started home, the bachelor and I headed to the house together. Pete had told me he was a weird duck, but he seemed ok to me always jokin around and clownin. When we got to the house, the Mrs. had cooked a hell of a supper!! Chicken fried steak, potatoes, gravy, corn, and apple pie!! When he came into the house, the bachelor sniffed then turned and went to his room. We waited supper a few minutes thinkin he was cleanin up or somethin. When he didn't return, I went to his door and knocked. He hollered: come on in. There he sat on his bedroll eatin a cheese sandwich!! I told him supper was waitin, but he shook his head and said he couldn't eat it. When I ask why, he said it sure smelled good but that he didn't believe in spendin money on food that way!! I told him he hadn't, and we let no one eat sandwiches while we ate a meal like that, and not be concerned with the cost. He still refused to eat with us sayin, "Eatin is a habit and you can break it if you try hard enough!" Well from then on, until he left, the Mrs. wouldn't speak to him. He ate cheese sandwiches and rolled grain from the feed mill, which he put sugar and milk on for cereal!! I never knew if he broke the habit but then I wasn't about to try myself!!

AZL's Old Goat

When I worked for AZL in the early 70s, they bought a big cow outfit in Florida, craziest cattle we ever saw. The joke around was the gaters made'm crazy! After about six months, the higher ups decided that that ranch needed an Arizona cow boss. Chas was given the duty. He was a good, young man with a lot of cow experience but all in the west!! But he was up for the challenge. He recruited a double handful of good Arizona cowboys who felt they were better than a bunch of whip crackin, web-toed, cracker cowboys. One was Kenny. Now Kenny was a little rowdy... no he was a lot rowdy!! The super at Hughes and Ganz, where I was, was a guy in his mid-50s who had married a very attractive young lady of 20 or so. Well everyone there teased him about bein an old goat chasin after that young girl and marryin her. Kenny made it real plain that it was sinful and he oughta repent!! So HE could have her!! That didn't go over well with the super!! Now the super was a hell of a guy for someone his age, you would have to look close to tell he was 40!! Now me and this super was good friends, we roped together, and socialized and such. And to be honest this cute young thing he was married to was a problem. She had a bad attitude toward the hired help and made life for hubby a pretty miserable affair. So when Chas recruited Kenny to go to Florida, the super breathed a sigh of relief. One less problem to deal with and no more daily harassment callin him an old goat.

When Chas and the boys got to Florida, they found this palmetto ranch stocked with red, brahmer cross cows that acted like deer, and a good sized heard of wild boars, along with a small bunch of goats that had gone wild. Kenny called back a couple times and gave us report on how things were progressing. It didn't sound like too much fun, sink holes, gaters, big snakes, and everything rotting from the moister and humidity.

After a month or so, Kenny called to say he was loadin out a load for Hughes and Ganz and on the truck there was a present for the super. Two days later, I was unloadin this truck from Florida. When the end gate was opened, a BIG red bull roared down the chute, kicked at my horse as he went by, ran onto the scales, promptly jumped the back gate, and continued on about his way!! I asked the weigh master if he caught the weight, but he failed to see the humor! While the other cowboys were trying to entice the red bull to come join the party, I continued unloading the truck. When the last animal was off, I loped the cattle to the scales and shut the gate on them. As I looked back, the driver at the truck was wavin me back. I loped back to him and he handed me an envelope addressed to the super. OK, now what? Off the truck came the stinkinest old billy goat I ever saw!! My horse liked the smell less than me and left there at a dead run!! When I got my horse under control, I opened a pen on one side of the alley and let that goat into it. I told the water trough washer to feed that goat some hay and I set off for the office to deliver the envelope.

When the super opened the envelope, his face got red, then white, and he started shakin. He got up and looked out the window at that goat from Florida, looked at me and said: get rid of him. How, I asked. I don't care, he said, turn him loose, eat him, I don't care!!!

I never knew what Kenny wrote in that note, but it took me a week to find someone to give that goat to. I think he ended up in some tacos!!!

New Shirt

The stockyards complex in Phoenix was a heck of a deal: a sale barn, a livestock supply store, office complex, bank, and the Stockman's Steak House!! Next to the sale barn was a little greasy spoon cafe that was run by Buster's wife. So, twice a day, we cowboys would go to the cafe and hang out. Breakfast was almost always a fried egg sandwich and lunch was a special or a burger. When done eating, we migrated to the livestock supply store which was operated by a local team roper. We would hang around shootin the bull and fingerin bridle bits, runnin our hands over new saddles and such. We all bought our ropes there, work types or arena. Now, in those days, when you bought a new rope it was pulled off a coil to the length you desired and you took it home, tied the knots and honda, sewed your own burner. Everyone knew how to do it.

This one day, Buster had bought a ready-made rope, one of the first I ever saw. Now, Buster was a BIG man, not so tall, just big. Broad-shouldered, deep-chested, slim waist and biceps that bulged the sleeves of his shirt, almost to bursting. His hands looked like they were carved from a mesquite stump. He was known to be short tempered, although not as bad as in his youth. You see Buster was almost 70 when this happened. He took his new rope back to the feed yard and, as was the custom, tied it to the saddle horn where it stayed until wore out. Next mornin, while doctoring some sick cattle, Buster noticed the new rope had stranded. In other words, one of the three strands that make up a rope had broken. This was very dangerous as the other two strands had to carry the load of three. Now, a nylon rope is a great thing until it breaks. They stretch an unbelievable amount, but like a rubber band will break, and 30 feet of stretched nylon rope will hurt ya a lot!! Well, Buster trotted to the saddle house and got another rope and threw the new rope in the back of his truck.

At lunch, we were all talkin about how a new rope would get stranded, and we decided it was just a flaw in the manufacturing process. After lunch, we all trouped down to the livestock supply store. Buster brought the new rope. There, he gently laid it on the counter and explained to Tim, the roper manager, what happened and he would just take a refund or a length off a coil. Tim shook his head and told Buster he wouldn't refund or trade as he thought the rope had been cut on a pipe post when buster roped a steer. Buster assured Tim that wasn't the case and we all agreed and swore that Buster's story was true. Tim leaned forward into Buster's face and told Buster: you old son of a bitch, you don't know what you want!!

22

Buster's hand shot out and grabbed Tim's shirt at the neck. The back of Buster's neck was as red as a fire truck!! I had a good view! Buster's good right hand was balled up and was pulled back for a day-ending punch for Tim!! Before anybody knew what happened, Tim was scurrying out the back door and Buster had a handful of rags in his hand!!! Tim didn't come back for his shirt for a long time!! I heard later Toveras paid for the shirt to keep peace in the neighborhood!!

The Beginning

In the early 70s, I was pretty unsettled, divorced, the job I loved was gonna shift. I didn't wanna stay there, so I quit and kinda shuttled around. What I really wanted was to go down the road in the summer on a run up through Colorado, Wyoming, and Montana and rope. I didn't have a solid rope horse, but I figured I could make one in a few months, under the right circumstances. I worked on a contract branding crew for a while, and did some day work to fill in the empty spot. I found a good palomino horse that didn't cost a bunch and was started as a head horse. Now I just needed a place to put a finish on him. That opportunity came calling one Sunday morning in the form of AZL. Monday, I moved to Queen Creek, settled into a single wide trailer, settled the palomino in the barn, and Tuesday, went to work. AZL had an arena, practice steers, and you could practice four days a week. Perfect. After a few weeks practice, I felt ole Rabbit was ready for a cheap jackpot ropin, or two. Every Saturday night was a ropin at 35th and Baseline at a place called Ikes. This got to be a hangout. I could rope a lot for not a lot of money, and usually made a little.

There was a young Mexican kid who hung out with me when I wasn't workin. He never went home until he had to. He had a bunch of brothers and sisters and he was the smallest in the litter. I got to takin him with me when I roped somewhere. His dad was a cowboy there, also, so naturally Carlos wanted to rope, too. It wasn't long until it became evident he was a natural. One spring evening, Carlos and I were at Ikes. I was lettin Carlos warm up my horse while I fished around for partners. Parked at the fence was a '66 El Camino with a blanket on the hood and on the blanket two of the pretties gals

I ever saw. Well, before the ropin was over, I had a date afterwards to take them for coffee. One, the blonde, jabbered like her jaw was unhinged. The other, a brunette, you couldn't pry a word out of. My little travelin partner wasn't happy with this deal at all. And as I found out later these gals thought Carlos was my kid!! But, as time went on, we straightened everything out. And as I kept seein this cute brunette, I started forgettin about that trip north!! Well, the up shot was, by summers end, that cute brunette and I were married. That started a life of rodeos, ranches and feedlots, three kids, a lot of misery, but a lot of good times. I never regretted for a minute not goin north. THAT was the beginning!!

Hughie

Hugh wasn't from Arizona. I'm not sure where he was from, but he was a good hand in the feedlots and in the rodeo arena. The only place I actually got to work with him was on a contract branding crew one winter, but I had been around him at feedlot ropins and various jackpot ropins. He was likable and always had a big toothy smile.

There was a time in the early 70s that the guys who wanted to rodeo worked on a contract crew brandin cattle in the feedlots around Arizona. You got paid by the head and, at a time when day wages was around 25 dollars a day, you could knock down a hundred or more per day. You had to be on a crew who was willing to work and work hard. You put in a lot of hours to make that kinda money. Hugh and I were the only ropers on our crew, the rest were bronc riders.

We had put a twenty hour shift at a feed yard and shut down to get a hot meal and change clothes. Branding chute work at a feedlot is bloody, nasty work. We told the feedlot we would be back in twelve hours to start again. We dropped Hugh off at his little trailer that he rented. Then we all scattered to home for a hot shower and meal agreeing to meet again in eight hours.

After the shower, hot meal and a nap, we all piled into the pickup and started out, but Hugh was a no show. We wheeled by his little trailer to wake him up. When we pulled up, he was sittin on the front steps, his arms wrapped around himself. This was at midnight in January. Yes, Arizona isn't as cold as a lot of places in the winter, but at midnight in January, its cold!! Hugh was still wearin his nasty clothes his hair was stickin out from under his Resistal and he wasn't smilin as usual. As we pulled up, he got in and asked if we would take him by a Jack in the Box, he was hungry. We went through the drive-through and ordered a burger with coffee. After he ate, he told us what happened as we drove to work.

It seemed that when we let him off he found his house occupied. His friend, Donnie, had a girl he had picked up in a bar in Hugh's bed. They locked him out and wouldn't let him in. His truck keys were in the house, Hugh said he begged and pleaded but all those two drunks did was laugh at him!! Finally, Hugh gave up and went for a walk. He tried to get somethin to eat, but he was so nasty and smelled so bad no one would let him in!! When he got back to his house, he had had enough. He was gonna break a window to get in. That's when we pulled up. Poor guy was froze, hungry, nasty, and tired. We found out later that while he was out walkin, that Donnie and the floozy had left. Hugh had never tried the door when he got back!! He told us later the floozy's perfume was industrial strength and wouldn't wash out of his blankets!! When Donnie sobered up he apologized, but I don't think Hughie ever forgave him!!!

Sam and the Health Department

In the late 60s and early 70s, livestock pharmaceuticals were pretty primitive compared to today. I was workin at the T&C Cattle Co. in Maricopa. We were processing and feeding out 25 thousand Mexican steers every 120 days. That was before it was unhealthy to eat meat, especially fat meat.

When we processed cattle then we castrated bulls, branded and maybe gave two vaccines. If the cattle had grubs, they got a cup of pour on spilled on their backs. That was it!! We shipped the fats to a Swift plant in Tolleson, Herseth Pack in Phoenix, Crockett Pack in Phoenix, Arizona Beef in Phoenix and a dozen packing houses on Vernon Street in Los Angeles.

As the industry heated up, we began to hear about cattle with "measles." We never saw any cattle with red spots, but then we found out they were referring to carcasses with red spots. These red spots were tape worm larvae embedded in the tissue of beef. Then, they were hand-trimmed out of the carcass. Later, they were frozen solid to kill them. Well, the packing house people were screaming their heads off at the feedlots, who screamed back. Then the health department got involved. Well, they decided employees at the feedlots were defecating in the feed troughs and the cattle would eat the crap with tape worm eggs and the cattle got measles. So, all the feedlots were to install outhouses out in the yards. Some called the porta potty companies, others built them and, in the case of AZL, built brick outhouses. Toveras were the worst measle offenders, which no one could figure out why. The fact that 90 percent of our cattle were straight out of Mexico, was not considered. Working in the yards was an old Mexican man named Serafin, and yes I'm pretty sure he was illegal, but in them days no one thought anything of it.

One day Sam, the superintendent, called all the employees to the scale house. There, waiting for us, was a representative of the State Health Department. He gave us all a little speech about crapping in the feed trough and handed each of us a brown paper bag with a plastic sandwich bag inside. We were instructed to place in the sandwich bag a "specimen" and then place the plastic bag in the paper bag, label our names on the outside, and turn it into him the next day. Well, Serafin spoke no English and by the time it was translated to him his eyes got that deer in the headlight look!! To the rest of us, this was the biggest joke in years. How far-fetched it got was a mystery to all of us, but we were told to go along with it or lose our jobs.

Next day there were a dozen brown paper bags in a box on Sam's desk, all labeled and some were decorated quite artistically. But Serafin's was absent. As a matter of fact, Serafin was absent. We went to lookin for him and found him washing water troughs out in the pens. When asked about his bag he ignored the question. Sam was starting to get mad. Serafin turned his back on us and said in Spanish it was a unholy thing to do. Sam didn't want to lose Serafin, as he was dependable and a hard worker, but couldn't avoid the problem. We put Serafin in the pickup and drove to the scale house. Sam handed Serafin his bag and he handed it back, shaking his head. Sam told him in Spanish to take the bag, fill it, or we would tie up a leg and collect the desired sample ourselves!! A few minutes later the old man delivered the bag, head hanging.

Everyone was cleared, no tape worms resided at our yard. Then they came up with cattle wormer that worked and the problem went away, but Serafin was already gone, back to Mexico, said all them damn gringos were unholy!!

Clayton Drove Cadillacs

Clayton was a cowman of legend. He smoked big Havana cigars, wore the best clothes, talked loud no matter where he was, and was a first rate cowman. He bought cattle for Toveras feedlots, managed some of the biggest ranches in Arizona, and knew every cowboy, rancher, cattle feeder and truck driver by their first names. Always ready for a laugh, at your expense or his, it didn't matter. His wife, Delores, was one of the most beautiful women I've ever seen. When traveling the West buying cattle, she drove and Clayton kept his books and talked on one of the first satellite phones I ever heard of. He was a high roller of the first order.

Once when I was unloading trucks at night at the Maricopa yard, he called to tell me some instructions on a specific load of cattle, all at once he went to hollerin: watch out, watch out, oooooh look out!!!! When he settled down, I asked what the deal was. He said Delores was drivin and the California traffic had them surrounded like a bunch of piss ants!!

After I left Toveras, I got married and traveled around working ranches and other feedlots. One day, I woke up with no job, a wife and two kids, with one on the way. Somehow, Clayton got word and tracked me down. He had taken over the management of a bankrupt feed yard for a bank and needed help. He already had my friend Pete there, so I went to Arlington. Clayton always had good horses, real good horses. When I got moved in, I found I had my own horse corrals stocked with extra good two and three year old colts ready to start. I had plenty to do, and Clayton checked on me daily to see how his colts were doin and to make sure I wouldn't pull the picket pin and move on. He didn't know it, but I was stayin as long as he would let me.

That summer, the dust in that feed yard was horrible. The cattle were getting sick on it, as well as the employees who lived there.

Clayton, somewhere, got a hold of an 8000 gallon Euclid water pull, a big tank with a motor on it!! Not many people knew how to run that thing, but they broke in a young Mexican boy who was settlin the dust as fast as he could. Clayton had just bought a new Cadillac, as pretty a car as you could ever hope to see. He picked it up in Phoenix and drove straight to the yard, parked in front of the scale house, and was talkin to Pete and me when around the corner came the Euc. That Mexican kid slowed down then turned off the key in preparation to stop. One problem: you turn off the key, EVERYTHING ceases to work!!! No brakes, no steering, nothin!! The tires on that thing were eight feet tall and they just kept rollin... right over the top of that new Cadillac!! Smashed to about four foot tall, with black tire tread down the middle from trunk to hood. We looked at Clayton, his cigar was dangling at about six o'clock, a fire in his eye was starting to ignite!! Pete looked at me and simply said time to go, we went. Clayton drove a pickup for a week or so until his special order car came in. The Mexican kid disappeared, and all vehicles were to park across the yard in a safe place!!

Sam and the DEQ

The old T&C Cattle Co. feedlot lay along the highway between Maricopa and Casa Grande. When it was built, there was very little traffic on that road. The Southern Pacific rail line ran through there, as it had for a hundred years. It no longer stopped train in Maricopa, but the water towers still stood when I was a kid. Maricopa was a junction in the old days, with a spur line running to the new farming community of Phoenix. Well, the spur line closed down and the roadbed became Maricopa road, in my youth, a two-lane asphalt road. Today, it is a four-lane divided highway.

When I worked at the T&C, the Casa Grande highway was only traveled by farm folks goin shoppin in Casa Grande. There were some farm houses in the vicinity, but the people who lived there were only cotton farmers. Well, that was the attitude we took. Never mind I grew up in a cotton farming household. Hell, I worked for a cow outfit, I was one of them. A fact of life around a feedlot was in the summer when the sun went down and the air started to cool, those fat cattle would get to buckin and bawlin and playin. 25 thousand of those would raise quite a dust cloud which was made up of manure, dried and powdered. To those of us used to it, we just smelled cash. To those with sensitive olfactory senses, it stunk!!

Sam was the boss at T&C, no question about it, the boss. We all loved workin for him because he let you cowboy, you weren't just a farmer on a horse, you were a cowboy. Sam had a temper, was cocky, and liked to play and joke, hard. He didn't put up with whining or complaining, but do the best you could and he gave you every break. Loyalty to the company was expected, and the company earned it. Sam saw to it. Sam worked you hard, long hours, and sometimes you might think he took advantage of you, but somewhere down the road he paid it back in triplicate.

One afternoon we, the crew with Sam, had finished sorting some fat cattle and were lounging in the scale house drinkin soda pop and tellin rodeo tales. I was too young to tell any, but I ate up the ones Sam, A.D., and Gilbert told. They had known Buckshot Sorrels, Hugh Bennit, and untold others who were legendary. We were aware of some the neighbors complaining about the dust in the evening, but we had a sprinkler system that kinda worked. Besides, we didn't tolerate whiners. While sittin there slurpin soda, a white sedan with State Government plates pulled up outside and a gray-haired fella in a black suit got out. He walked into the scale house and looked around, nodded, and turned to Sam, who was behind the desk. "Do you know where I could find Ed Tovera, Harold Christopherson, or Sam White?" he asked.

Sam grinned and said: I dont know, do ya have warrants for them? The old man said "I very well may have!!"

Sam set up put his feet on the floor and asked who the old man was. The fellow produced a badge and a set of papers. At that, the rest of us made a retreat out the back door!!!

As it turned out, he was from the State Department of Environmental Quality. He was there to put a stop to the dust that rose out of that feedlot every night. Well, the bottom line was the company bought two water trucks and rigged them to spray into the pens as they were drivin along. It took a good month before the dust settled enough to see a difference. We cowboys often had to drive those trucks, something we sure didn't like, but Sam said do it, so we did.

A.D. Lost His Thumb

When I was at Toveras, there was a cowboy there who I kinda looked up to. He was as good a cowboy and horseman as you could hope to ask for. He had trained race horses, rodeoed, run ranches, and lived a wild raucus life. Trouble was, that wild raucaus life was mostly illegal!!

His name was A.D. He liked to tell people it stood for 'after death'!! He drank whiskey like water, dipped Copenhagen snuff, cussed a blue streak, and was generally a pain in the butt, but he was a cowboy. He was prematurely gray-headed, about six foot tall and lean as a whip. Tom T. Halls song Faster Horses was written about A.D.; if it wasn't, it should have been!! A.D. was a team roper, a damn good one, header or heeler made no difference. I've seen him rope for weeks and not miss a loop. His horses were fast, quick, and deadly. They had to be because his temper was a terrible thing to behold, man or beast!!

A.D.'s pride and joy was a sorrel, bald-faced, stocking-legged gelding named.... you guessed it SOCKS!! When heading in the arena, Socks could run a hole in the wind and get you to a steer so fast you couldn't get your loop up quick enough. The minute you turned that loop loose, he was sliding his left hind foot and running on the other three feet turning that steer almost as fast as he was running forward. He was still a young horse, and basically still learning, but he made that turn at full speed on his own. If the loop was to miss, there was no way to bring him back in line with the steer.

We were practicing one afternoon when a A.D. roped a big steer and was dallying as Socks went left, only this time A.D.'s thumb got caught in the rope and, with Socks speed and the weight of the steer, that thumb came off just like a knife had cut it off.

Sam's pickup was parked close, so we loaded A.D. in the middle and headed to the hospital 18 miles away. As we went by Sam's house, he stopped, ran in, and returned with a bag of ice and a pint of whiskey. We wrapped the hand in a towel and packed the ice around the mangled thumb. As we drove out the gate, Sam handed the whiskey to A.D. asking if he needed some. He was white as a sheet and shook his head no. THAT was the only time I ever saw him turn down a drink!! But, he had a healthy pull from that jug by the time we reached the hospital!! Sam said he didn't think he was that bad off!

Sasabee

On the Mexican border, southwest of Tucson, is a small border village of Sasabee. The only commerce there is the ranches on each side of the border. It is remote to both Mexican and American alike. On the Mexican side, one of the ranches is owned by the Osuna family. For generations they have ranched there and worked on the American side for added income.

One of the Osuna family, Pablo, was a good friend of mine. He worked at a different feedlot than me, but we roped together at different ropins and socialized. He had a large family and was always scrappin up side deals to keep the many mouths fed, plus I was told he helped support his brother at the ranch in Mexico. Pablo was always mounted on, if not the best lookin horses, the best handling and best trained. I saw a mule he trained once. That mule handled like a horse: could spin, slide, and work a cow like no other. When asked where he got the mule, Pablo smiled and pointed south. He would periodically come up with some really nice young horses. He would get them broke then sell them for what was, at the time, a good amount of money. I remember a little palomino mare about 14 hands and a thousand pounds. She was catty quick and could run a hole in the wind for about 150 yards. Pablo roped on her and cut cattle on her. She was a doll. I asked him, again, one day where he got her. Again, he smiled and pointed south.

About a month later, he asked me to drive him to Sasabee to see his brother. Would I pull his trailer, he asked. Sure, why not. When we were a mile from Sasabee, Pablo had me turn off on a two track trail that led along the international fence. About two miles into the trip, the road died at a big mesquite thicket. Pablo jumped out, squatted down, and pointed into the thicket. There I could see three sets of horse's legs. Pablo whistled and a young Mexican boy riding one horse's bareback and leading two more came up to the truck. Pablo explained that the boy was his nephew and that the horses were from the family ranch across the line. How did they get here, I asked. He smiled and told me to follow him. The nephew rode his pony back into the thicket. We followed. In the middle of the thicket was a hole sloping down into the ground. It was paved in concrete and after walking down the ramp you could tell it was a tunnel that was built to accommodate a truck. Pablo explained that during prohibition the whiskey smugglers built it and used it to run whiskey into Tucson. When prohibition was repealed, it was forgotten and the Osuna family had their own port of entry. They took horses and cattle both ways through the tunnel.

I saw Pablo a few years ago and asked, with all the activity along that part of the border, if they still used the old tunnel. He shook his head in a sad way and said, no, the border patrol found it and blew it up. No mas, he said as he shook his head.

Branded

Years ago, I was workin on a contract branding crew to kinda fill-in between ridin jobs. Cleve was the boss and a heck of a good guy to work for. He was quiet, fair, and doin his best to keep body and soul together. He had a nice young family, a pretty wife, and a couple little kids. We were puttin in a lot of hours. A couple times I remember workin 30 hours straight through. There were a lot of cattle traded at that time and it wasn't unusual for us to process the same bunch of cattle two or three times as they changed hands on the same day!

Some owners had electric irons and some had propane-heated stamp irons. Workin around a branding chute is a nasty, bloody job, and after you spend a day or so workin up to a thousand head of cattle through a chute, you're a mess!! I always wore my worst clothes and, after a work shift, would soak them in a tub of cold water overnight before washing them. They were blood stained permanently, the pockets tore or missing, and big holes in the knees of the Wranglers.

One day it was a cold, raw day with a wind whippin in under the shed the chute sat in. We had a big roaring propane-fed fire heating the irons. Now, Cleve usually sat in the bull hole castrating the bull calves as they came through the chute. The rest of us dehorned, vaccinated, ear tagged, etc. One hand kept the cattle pushed up the lead up to the squeeze, we never ran out of cattle. Periodically, I would have to mix vaccine in enough quantities to keep the crew movin. One day I was a bit slow in reloading the vaccine guns, with my back to the chute, I was concentrating on the chore at hand when I felt a warm localized source of heat. I jumped and looked back.

Cleve was grinnin at me with a red-hot iron in his hand. The pocket on my Wranglers was gone. Only one thickness of fabric protected my posterior!! We all had a laugh and went back to work.

A few days later, I was presented the opportunity to repay the prank. Well, Cleve's pants had a pocket and I had to leave that Number 6 iron there a little longer than he did mine. Finally, he squalled and jumped straight up fannin his butt!!

A few days later, we all went dancin at a local bar and dance hall. Cleve's wife and I were dancin and she got to laughin. I ask what was so funny. She told me thank you for permanently identifying her husband. I ask what she was talkin about. She explained that number "6" I branded him with peeled, and now she could tell, even in the dark, he was hers!!!

Ed McFarkle

When I got to AZL, there was a heck of a crew already working there. Only a couple were cowboys, the rest were wannabes. Bud and Dude were real top hands. Jerry was my age and as single and as I was and we rode together, a good hand. Then there was Ed.

Ed was in his sixties, a heavy smoker and drinker. He had been a top rodeo hand in the 40s and 50s. He wasn't very big, maybe 5'4" and, if he weighed 110 pounds, I'll eat my hat. He had been a racehorse's trainer in the Northwest. His health wouldn't let him stay in that wet country, so he came back to Arizona to get his lungs dried out, except those unfiltered cigarettes were wreaking havoc on him. I don't know if he had ever been married, he didn't say. He still liked to rope and was after someone every week to go rope with him at a jackpot. The problem was he was drunk before the ropin was over, and if you were in his truck, he wouldn't let you drive. I only went with him one time like that, that was enough!! He would be drivin along, suckin on a beer, smokin a cigarette, and get to caughin. When that happened, there was no tellin where his little truck would go!! How we got back without gettin killed, I'll never know. Because of that hackin cough, everyone got to callin him McFarkle. He drove a Datsun pickup with a two horse trailer. His rope horse, called Leo, was a trailer fighter. I wonder why. When he got to hackin, almost immediately ole Leo would go to scramblin in the trailer with Ed sayin "wa wa wa stand up Leo!"

We had been to a ropin one night and started home when Ed decided we needed to stop at a bar on South Mountain. You had to drive up a steep driveway to get to the bar. We started up that grade pullin two horses with a Datsun pickup with a four-cylinder motor!! After down shifting three times, we stalled about a third of the way up. We started to roll backward slowly with Ed hacking, Leo scramblin, and me tryin to figure out how I would explain my presence in a hospital to my new boss and my folks!! But thanks to the drunk gods, we coasted into an empty parking lot, jackknifing the trailer to a stop. Ed sat there in a stupor and finally looked up and said he needed a new truck because this one wouldn't get him to the bar!! I was about ready to unload my horse and ride home!! But Ed was done for the night so I got to drive. That was never going to happen again!! From then on, if Ed wanted to go he went in my truck with me drivin!! Then he bought a new full-size Dodge pickup. When behind the wheel, you just saw Ed's hat. He got stopped a few times for that!! Ed left there the next year and we never knew where he ended it up, but he left a legacy that went on for a while!!

Tail Gates are Dangerous

Over the years, I've seen this happen numerous times with results from a scratch to unconsciousness and stiches.

I was working in the Tovera yard in Phoenix. One of the principals there raised registered Charlois cattle on the side. One Saturday afternoon, I was the only one at the yard just puttin in my time. There was a kid there whose daddy was a feed truck driver. He was hangin out, waitin for his dad to get off work. Harold, the owner of the registered cattle, called the scale house and asked if I would take the company pickup and trailer to the sale yard and pick up a bull that had been mistakenly left there. Since I was twiddlin my thumbs any way, I agreed to the chore. Billy, the kid, wanted to go and I saw no problem with that. We would only be gone a few minutes. The truck was a Chevy short-bed pickup and the trailer was a bumper-pull Hale stock trailer with wooden slates bolted in place.

When we got to the sale barn, not a soul was to be found. We sat the trailer in place to load the bull and went lookin for him. After a few minutes, we found Mr. Bull, locked in a dry corral about as big as a postage stamp. Mr. Bull had been there a couple days, no water, no feed. When I open the gate, he came at us like a locomotive, hooked his head at me as he thundered by. I had stepped behind the gatepost and, as the bull headed up the alley, I fell in behind a joggin along. Little Billy was sittin on the fence at the trailer out of harm's way. As we got close to the trailer, I yelled at the bull who broke into a run with me right on his heels at a dead run. As the bull jumped into the trailer, I swung the tail gate shut as the bull was switching ends in the trailer. Then the lights went out.

When I came around, I was sittin on the ground at the end of the trailer, the bull was still in the trailer, the gate was latched, Billy was washing my face with a wet rag. My head felt like a trip hammer was going inside.

Billy said the bull had hit the end gate as I shut it, the gate hitting me in the forehead. He said I latched the gate and then sat down. I had a three-inch hole in my forehead where one of the bolts in the tailgate had tapped me between the eyes!! The wet rag Billy was bathin my face with was saturated in blood.

After unloading the bull, back home, Billy's dad drove me to a local emergency room where I got a tetanus shot and five stiches in my head. I ate aspirin for a week before that trip hammer shut down. I was lucky. I've known truckers, loading fat cattle, who have teeth knocked out, jaws broken, and one lost an eye. I saw a horseshoer helping load a bronc get slammed in the face with a kicked tailgate. So, folks watch them tailgates. They are dangerous!!

Promotion

When President Nixon was in office, he and his economic people decided that the industry in the US needed to stop giving raises and perks. This was supposed to help the economy. That little idea didn't last long, but it came at a time when feedlot cowboys were struggling financially and needed every dime we could earn.

When the freeze was put on, there was a bunch of us at Toveras that were pretty put out. We hadn't had a raise in two years and the cost of living was creeping up daily. Besides, entry fees at rodeos and jackpots were goin up!!

The owners sent word down through Sam that there would be no raises. I remember him turning red in the face, his hands shakin, and his temper taking control for a short period of time. We all wanted to be someplace else, real quick, but Sam would have none of it. He grabbed a phone and in just a few seconds he had Mr. Tovera on the line. He reminded him of our loyalty, and how we had been promised raises. He listened for a half minute or so, his face getting redder. Then, in a quiet but firm and stern voice said, "If I loose one man over this, I'm going with him." Then he hung the phone up and looked at all of us and told us he didn't blame us if we all walked out. Before he finished, the phone was ringing. Sam answered, listened for a second or so, said goodbye and hung up. "Bookkeeper be here tomorrow, boys. Will ya hang til then?" We all agreed to wait until the bookkeeper got there. I don't think any of us had planned to leave, but no one vocalized it.

Next day when the bookkeeper got there, Sam called us all into the scale house to hear what he said. The bookkeeper had studied the ruling and said he found a loop hole: if you got promoted to a more responsible position you could receive a raise in pay. So, Gilbert was promoted from pen rider to head of the shipping dept. Pete was promoted from pen rider to head of the processing department. I was promoted from barn manager (colt breaker) to pen rider! And A.D. was promoted to water truck manager. In this way, we all got our fifty-dollar-a-month raise!! Now this was all on paper because none of us changed what we had been doin for four years. Ya know the sad thing, I don't think Sam got a raise, but he was ready to go to bat for the rest of us!!

Colts

When I got out of high school, I didn't want to work the summer away on the cotton farm my Dad ran. I had a bellyful of hoeing weeds, irrigating cotton, and other miserable jobs that I felt were fit for lower classes of folks!! But I had no other choice. That's all there was in my hometown at the time: cotton. There were a couple feedlots goin in, but my chances of goin to work there were slim and none; or so I thought. One night, the phone rang and it was for my Dad. When he got off the phone, he let us in on what was goin on. You see, in those days you didn't eavesdrop on someone's phone conversations; not in our house anyway, not if you knew what was good for you.

It seems the manager at Toveras, or T&C Cattle Company as it was called, needed someone to start some colts. If it worked out, I would have a part-time job when I went to school in the Fall. My Dad had told Sam that he could get by without me, as I was worthless as a cotton farmer.

My Dad and Mom went to church with Sam and Helen, the manager at Toveras. Sam had seen some colts I had started in high school and thought I would be alright. Well, I went to work with a Porter's saddle, a hackamore, and a know-it-all attitude. Boy was I in for an education. Sam White knew more ways to gentle a colt and put a finish on one than almost anyone I met before or since. Lots of top-notch horse trainers started out working for Sam, then moved on to greater things. I can't say that about me, but I had some success with my horses. I, over the years, showed some horses, having the state champion stallion two years running, and qualified him to the national show in all the cattle events. This was with the things I learned working for Sam breaking colts. Sam would come to the round corral and sit there as I worked with a green colt talking to me. Without knowing it, I was doing things Sam wanted me to do and learning all the time.

I also found Sam to be a prankster, a rough prankster. I would spend a week in the round pen with a colt, get a ride or two in, then slip them outside. Now there was no open country thereabouts. It was across an asphalt road in front of the barn and 100 yards up it to the main gate into the feedlot, the scale house set just beyond there. It had great big windows overlooking the yard and down the road to the horse barn. The first colt I took out of the round pen and started up the road to the yard was snorty, skittish, and temperamental. He had already runaway with me in the round pen to the point we both got dizzy, but I thought I had him ready to go. As I almost got to the gate, I looked up and here came Sam rollin a metal garbage can right at us!! Old colt stood for that about five seconds and we left, headed back to the barn!! I just went along for the ride; seemed like the thing to do at the time. It took me another week to get that colt back up that road, every time he would snort stamp his foot and, if he couldn't run off, would run backwards!! All this time, Sam was laughin himself silly, but I got even.

We were weighin fat cattle one mornin. The last five steers wouldn't take the last step onto the scales. Two of us a horseback were pushin the gate as hard as we could, our horses shoulderin into the gate and us hollerin and cussin. Sam came out of the scale house with a hot shot. He handed me the handle end with him holdin the business end. When I grabbed the handle I got ahold of the button. Ole Sam let loose real quick!! He glared at me with fire in his eye. I smiled and said sorry. After a second, he smiled and said were even. Over the next six years, I started all the colts there with the exception of one crop when I was in the service, and what colts they were. Two full brothers were Rebel Cause, Tonto Bar Gill bred. Both went to the track and could run a hole in the wind, the oldest one winning the consolation at the All-American. Some were foundation bred quarter horse, Buzzy Bell H, Tony, Music Mount, Pelican, and Hancock. Mares were bred to Rebel Cause, Vangard, Little Request and a little Leo-Yellow Wolf stud that came from New Mexico. He was just a cow pony stud but I think his colts were probably the best of the bunch.

When I found out by mistake that Sam was leaving, I didn't see any sense in staying. Never since have I run into a cow outfit, feed yard, or ranch with such horses. Of course, I guess it's easy to look back and say they were the best, but I'll always believe they were.

The Great Potato Stampede

While I was at Hughes and Ganz, a division of AZL, we had a couple of great big pens about a half mile away from the main yard, down behind the hay barns. These were called the pasture pens, and together they would hold almost a 1000 head of steers. We never put anything down there that wasn't half-finished because it was a problem doctoring fresh cattle there. Chances of half-finished cattle getting sick was small and they were less problems, unless you don't count taking them there from the main yard. There was no fenced lane of any kind from the main yard that half mile to the pens. The gate that allowed access was small—a ten footer—and it was in the middle of the fence, the hardest kinda deal to put cattle through.

The road down there was a one lane affair elevated between two irrigated potato fields.

Word came down that we were gonna send a fresh batch of cattle down there. It would take a combined crew from section one and two-twelve men. You would think that would be enough, but not quite. The section boss from section two was to empty the pens at the main yard and send the cattle down an alley to the rest of us waiting outside. The wise thing to do would be take them in one, or two, hundred head lots, but oh no, Jack kicked the whole thousand out to us. Now those cattle got to buckin and bawlin and playing on dry powdery ground until you couldn't see your hand in front of your face. The section boss from section one came by me at a lope and told me he would take the lead to the pens down that little narrow road. I was to turn a 1000 head of silly, half-fat, crossbred steers down a ten-foot-wide road with irrigated potatoes on each side. The rest of the boys were doin all they could to hold these steers in one pile, let alone drive them. Then Jack showed up, went to hollerin, and rode right up the big middle of the herd at a trot: his intent was to put a bunch of leaders on the road so the rest would follow. With that much dust flying, no one saw that handful of steers take the road. Jack never looked back, just kept a hollerin and runnin those steers up the road. Two of the cowboys on the potato patch side saw what was goin on and spread the word to shove the cattle to the road all at once. I turned the leaders and the herd took the road, but that many cattle didn't fit. On each side of the road the steers spilled out into the fresh irrigated potatoes, tromping them into a muddy mess!! We tried to get them out but bogged our horses to the saddle skirts!! That bunch of steers churned up those potato patches then turned back to home. We held them, and before we could stop them they turned and once more stampeded into the potatoes. With the damage done, we charged the steers toward that ten-foot gate and the two men who were going to turn them in it. Some made the gate, most didn't and went on by. We got around them on dry ground and held them up until they settled down. By now, that wasn't too hard as those steers had pooped out. When they settled, they strung out like cattle should, walked to the gate and entered as calm as you please.

We know AZL had to pay for the potato crop, but we never heard how much. Potato chip potatoes didn't come cheap even then. From

39

then on, when cattle were moved to or from the pasture pens it was done when the fields were dry, and in in 100 head bunches!! Jack ended up a pickup driver and I got his job.

Arizona's Cowtown

Years ago in the early 60s, almost all the commercial feedlots in Arizona were concentrated in the Salt River Valley. Most were along 48th street in Phoenix starting at Washington and extending one after another South into the dry Salt River bed. Well, with one wet winter, a hundred year flood and the housing boom, it wiped them out: some to never reopen, most to relocate to other areas of the state.

The farmers in my hometown realized they could sell land to the feeders for new feedlots then sell feed staples they grew for the fatting of the cattle. The feeders who were interested in relocating to the area wanted some sort of guarantee that somewhere down the line that people moving in close to the feedlots wouldn't be able to file lawsuits to move them out. The farmers, in conjunction with the feeders, went to the state legislature and requested a special zoning of a township for feedlots and packing houses. It was granted and construction began on the first feedlot, T&C Cattle Co., an extension of the Tovera family.

Soon Smith and Kelly followed, then Producers. South, at the far end of the township, John Wayne and Lewis Johnson built the famed Red River Feed Lot. Cudahy bought land to build a new packing house between Smith and Kelly and T&C. Things were moving along well until the farmers got greedy: they ran the prices on the ground in the township out of sight so that other cattle feeders turned their backs and bought land in other parts of the state. Mcelhany built theirs in Wellton, Hughes and Ganz in Queen Creek, Spur Feeding was built on an Indian lease at Santan, Olen Dryer built in Laveen and Goodyear.

When the cotton growers woke up to the fact they weren't going to sell any more dirt, they went screaming to the capital to have the zoning on the cowtown township changed!! I was working at T&C when the state legislature bus came through the feed yards on tour. After visiting with everyone at every feedlot and getting the feel for the situation, they adjourned to their hallowed halls to consider the situation. Those cotton farmers were rubbing their greedy hands in anticipation of the ruling. Land developers had never lost a decision where feedlots were concerned.

After a couple weeks, the committee handling the matter handed down the ruling: the cowtown township would remain as it was set up for 100 years!! When the farmers and land developers complained, they were told: this was what you wanted in the first place so live with it!! They could still sell their land for homes, but the buyers had to sign an agreement that they understood about the disposition of the feed lots. And, so it remains today. Yes, there are houses in the area, but to my knowledge there has been no movement to push the cattle feeders out.

I Dont Hire ###$$@@##$ Team Ropers!!!!

Ya know, I've always roped. Everywhere I went or worked, I roped, but the job came first. If it came down to a good job and going to a ropin, I stayed and worked. If it was a bad job, welll let's just say that was whole different kettle of fish.

In those years, I worked for Toveras and AZL, and they spoiled me. They furnished arenas and cattle for their employees, and were generally supportive of a man who competed under the company name. While working for AZL, I qualified for the world feedlot championships twice. Voluntarily, we saved our vacation time for the trip to the finals. They, in return, would help out financially to some extent. They liked to brag about us doin well.

But there were a lot of feeders who took a dim view of such goins on. It's funny, but they always had the worst managed yards and the poorest quality help. They wouldn't pay good wages and whined about everything. They would cheat the feed on their horses or had no horses at all. If they had horses, they were generally the chicken feed type, cheap to buy and non-productive.

I had fair job where I was, a nice comfortable house and some security, but I had gone up the ladder as far as I was gonna go. Nice people to work for but due to family concerns, the upper tier of jobs weren't going to be available to the hired help. Well, word came to me that a local cattle feeder had fired his yard manager. I knew the fired manager and knew he knew the business, but he was prone to party for days at a time, run around on his wife, and was a regular rounder. He roped, but was seldom in the money because he was too busy drinkin and girlin.

I put in a call to this cattle feeder and told him I wanted to apply for the job. He agreed to meet me the next day at his office. When I arrived at this prominent gentleman's office, I had a couple of letters of recommendation and was dressed in my best cowboy attire. When showed into the office, this gentleman rose to shake hands, then looked down at the gold buckle on my belt. His face turned red, he started shakin, and froth came to the corners of his mouth.

"Get out!" he yelled. I was stunned. I tried to speak, but instead this old man went into a screamin fit. "You goddamn team ropers. All you do is get drunk, beat your horse and cheat on your wives! Get out now!"

I left as disappointed and deflated as you could get. That night Clayton, one of the fellows who wrote a letter for me, called me to see how things went. He listened, quietly, while I explained how the short interview went. When I was done, Clayton said he thought the guy that just got fired might have ruined the deal with his antics. Clayton told me not to worry because even though the job paid more I wouldn't have been happy for long. Maybe there was a reason the other fella drank and raised hell so much. As time went on, I saw that cattle feeder trade yard bosses pretty regular. They usually quit. So maybe that gold buckle saved me a hard lesson.

Dude, Bugs, and the Ferrari

While at AZL, the super got a wild bug and went out and bought a Ferrari sports car: fire engine red, six inches off the ground, and 0 to 900 in 6.3 seconds. Just what ya need to cruise around a feedlot. At the office, he had a carport built to accommodate the hot little Italian job. He would come to work, park the car and then use a company pickup to show fat cattle to buyers.

Just to the north of the office was the horse barn and saddle house. It was paved with asphalt all the way to the offices. To the right was the feedlot, gravel feed alleys and cattle alleys. So the ride from saddle house to feed lot could be a little scary as you had a slick surface, feedlot feed trucks, hay trucks and all manner of vehicles cruising around. Not great for gentle horses, not to mention colts and broncs.

Dude was one of the cowboys there when I went to work there. After a couple years the company changed policy and would let the cowboys keep more than one personal mount. We all had our rope horses, but this change allowed us ride colts for other folks for pay, or buy a colt, train them and sell them for extra income. Dude went to our old friend Jack Clem and bought a little stag bronc. He had run as a stud until his eight-year-old year, was untouched by human hands prior to castration and was as waspy a little horse as you could ask for.

Dude kept this wild-eyed little hellion in a small solid walled little pen where there was no chance of him jumping out. Dude named his new pride and joy "BUGS," because he was bug-eyed. After a couple weeks of hard work, Dude moved Bugs to the horse barn with the rest of the horses. Bugs didn't buck much. Bugs was very unpredictable. Sometimes he would try to run away; sometimes he would simply sull and not move at all.

When shipping fat cattle, we always saddled our broke horses. Then when we were through we would go to the saddle house for coffee and change to our green colts to ride pens.

This one morning after coffee, Dude decided to saddle Bugs for a stint at checking pens. Bugs seemed docile as Dude saddled him. Dude had hobbled Bugs in the front of the saddle house. Bugs stood as a statue while Dude cinched his saddle to the little bay. When Dude turned to pick up his hackamore, Bugs farted, snorted, wheeled on his hind feet, and started bucking across the pavement towards the office. The hobbles weren't slowing him down at all. Dude broke into a run when he saw where Bugs was headed. There was no hope he could catch him before he reached the office, but Dude didn't know what else to do.

The red Ferrari was parked in its usual spot in the car port and Bugs was zeroed in like a radar-guided-missile!! I could hear Dude saying "oh shit, oh shit," as he ran after his horse. As Bugs came to the carport, he was in mid-air bawlin like a bull buffalo caught in a locomotive cow catcher. At mid-jump, the saddle horn on Dude's saddle caught the lip of the roof. This rattled the carport and jerked Bugs to the ground right behind the sports car!! Before the little bay could regain his feet, Dude landed on him like a hen on a clutch of eggs!! I caught up a horse back and Dude gave me the lead rope and let Bugs up. The little booger kept on trying to buck but snubbed to my saddle horn couldn't get unwound. We were trying to quietly get away from the office when the front door opened. Dude ducked his head as he knew what was coming. Mr. Super walked out real slow, not saying a word. He slowly walked around the car looking at it. When he reached the front fender and found no damage, he looked at Dude and asked if Dude was going to sell Bugs. Dude assured him he would. Mr. Super simply turned and went into the office and shut the door. Dude wilted. I thought he would pass out. Sure enough, he sold Bugs three months later and made a handsome profit. But at that time he still wasn't shod, and was never allowed near red sports cars!!

Colt Starter

While workin for T&C Cattle Co., it was my job to start the colts each fall that the company had raised for the cowboys to use in the feed yard. After 60 days or so, they would each take one to add to their string. Feed yard work is hard on horses and the lameness factor is high. There were always three or four broke horses turned out for one reason or another. So every horse was needed in turn.

A lot of funny things happened while I was startin colts. One of them was a feller showed up lookin for work. We were shorthanded, so Sam put him on, told him be there next mornin at 5 a.m. New hand showed up at 6, not good. Sam was death on being late to ship fat cattle. Sam showed this cat his horses, told him shake a leg, jumped in his truck, and rushed back to the scale house. I was in the round pen with a colt. Now this round pen was made out of railroad ties stood on end, side by side. There was a little crack between the ties, but other than that it was a solid wall. Pretty soon, I heard someone clear his throat. Lookin around I couldn't see anyone. Again, the sound came and I realized someone was peeking between two ties. I walked over and the new man asked me to help him. I thought he had a serious problem, so I left my colt and walked over to the barn with him. On the ground was a new Sears and Roebuck saddle with a new cotton blanket; a cheap Jap import bit on a cardboard headstall lay in the dirt next to it. I asked what the problem he needed help with was. He pointed to the rig on the ground and asked if I would show him how to use it!! I almost passed out because I had heard him tell Sam what a whampus kitty cowpuncher he was. I looked around to see who was watchin, then as fast as I could, saddled his horse and beat a fast retreat to the round pen. This clown never untracked his horse, just crawled on and wallered him around and ambled toward the scale house.

I stayed busy in the corral the better part of the mornin and was takin a breather squatted down next to the fence in the shade when someone above me told me I wasn't gettin much done sittin there. I looked up and Sam was grinnin at me from on top of his horse. I straighten out and pointed to the colt in the middle of the pen, drippin with sweat and told Sam he was on strike.

Sam set there a minute and finally looked me in the eye and asked if I saddled the gunsels horse. I told him I had. He asked why I hadn't said anything to him about it. I told him: in the first place I hadn't seen anyone until now, and secondly, I figured he would figure it out. Sam laughed and told me I was right and would I please go turn those horses he assigned that clown out, he had already left. Didn't take long with Sam. Try your best, tell him the truth, and he would help you all day long. Lie to him or be lazy you were down the road.

Chasin Ole Crooked Horn

When I worked for Toveras, they had pastured some steers with an outfit that had irrigated pasture next to the Gila River Indian Reservation. The Gila River passes through the middle of that land, and growing along its banks for miles is a little patch of mesquite forest called the New York Thicket. It is one of the largest, continuous mesquite thickets in Arizona, maybe the Southwest. The river is usually dry, but in protected places water comes to the surface for short distances. When Toveras shipped off the irrigated pasture, they found they were short 50 head or so. These had ended up in the thicket. There were already an untold number of escapee cattle there, not to mention hundreds of wild horses. Toveras put a 50 dollar bounty on the steers they were missing, so when we got a day off, some of us went to the river to try to get a little reward money.

This one particular Sunday afternoon, the old timer and myself were prowling in the thicket. The tracks were thick and the cow sign was everywhere. We started tracking this one bunch of cattle down river, and as we entered a clearing there would be a little dust hanging in the air and maybe the smell of cow, we were that close. In the trail's powdery dust was one track that looked like a ski: long, narrow and it belonged to a big animal. As the day progressed we kept after this bunch hoping they would poop out. They never did. Dark found us six miles from our truck and a long, dry ride back. The next morning at the feedlot, we had weighed up the fat cattle to ship and were waiting for the brand inspector. His truck turned into the yard pullin an open top, bumper pull stock trailer. In this trailer, standing about a foot above the side boards, were two of the biggest steers I ever saw. One was a Herford, his head tied down to the floor board to keep him from jumping out. Next to him, and standing another foot taller than the Herford, was a crossbred Mexican steer. He had a four foot horn on one side and the horn on the other had been broken and turned down and grew under the steers neck and up to a point it almost touched the good horn on the other side!!

The old timer was looking around when something struck him and he looked at the steer's feet. Sure enough, that long toed track belonged to Ole Crooked Horn. When asked how they came by these steers the Indian brand inspector explained that a couple white cowboys had run them all day Sunday and when the moon came out he and another Indian cowboy had caught these cattle on an alkali flat!! Ole Crooked Horn had gored and killed one horse and hadn't given up very easy.

They took those steers to the old Paramount Packing House in Casa Grande and that Old Crooked Horn steer lived out his life there as a curiosity. The only brand that could be read on him was last used in 1948, the year of my birth!! That made that ole steer 21 years old when he was caught. As Maxwell Smart said, "missed him by that much!!"

Ranches

Florence

Years ago, I was helping Dave down at Alamo Lake. We spent a lot of time in camp. One night, just at dark, Joe Beeler and some other folks showed up for supper. Among them was Joe's daughter, just back from Italy and studying art there. When Dave ask what she was up to, she explained that the school wanted to send her to Florence for more studying. Dave said, "Hell, that ain't nothin. Arizona's been tryin to send me to Florence for years"!!!!

Bob Shoefly Shufelt

The last time I saw Bob "Shoefly" Shufelt, the great cowboy artist, was years ago at a brandin in Aguila, Arizona. We had been workin all day flankin calves together. It was hot and dusty and dry. We were sittin on an old, dry water trough takin a break when one of the punchers there, who wasn't much hand, started braggin about Texas. Bob unloaded on him. "I'll tell you about Texas. Little pastures of a 1000 acres, corrals built of pipe, and big ole hosses tied to a fence while they work their cattle through a calf table!! These Arizona cowboys gather 20 sections, put the cattle in a net wire corral and drag calves to the fire on the same 1000 pound horses they gathered on all day!! Don't tell me about Texas!!!"

Mrs. Jefe and the Bankers

YEARS AGO, MRS. JEFE AND I WERE GATHERING A BUNCH OF STEERS TO SHIP AT THE OX RANCH. THIS PARTICULAR DAY, the bankers were along. By 10 o'clock it was HOT! Now we never carried water, but these bankers kept whining about being thirsty. We had about 200 steers in the drive and was headed out of the pasture to the corrals. Every time the bankers asked about water, we just told them it was over the next ridge. Mrs. jefe was in the lead. When a windmill came in sight, the bankers were on the drags. The steers all lined up at the water trough with Mrs. jefe at the top end. From where we sat, the bankers thought she was drinkin out of the trough with the steers, they weren't very thirsty then. Actually, she was drinkin from the pipe at the mill!!!

Someone's Prowlin

Every year during round up, Mrs. jefe ALWAYS cooked chikin fried steak. Big meal, gravy, corn, biscuits, the whole works. We had a friend stayin with us. About 1 am Mrs. jefe woke me up. "Someone's prowlin the house," she says! I tipped-toed down the hall and there, in the kitchen, is my friend in his underwear cuttin a piece of steak. "Just one more chunk," he said!!

Crossin the Gila River Reservation

Years ago, when I was just a button, when school would let out for the summer, I would saddle my pony at daylight and head to Chandler to stay at my grandparents' house. It was a 30 mile ride, but in them days we didn't think much of it. One time, as I was crossin the Gila River Indian reservation, I ran onto a Indian cowboy goin my way. We rode together for a ways. Pretty soon we came across the old Snake Town site, a Hohokam site on the Gila River. The ground was a mosaic of broken pottery. My companion stopped his horse and looked around. "My family maybe live here," he said. "Ole lady get mad at the ole man and breakit allll the dishes!!!" With that, he turned his horse and rode off chucklin!!

Mr Rose

Mr. Rose was an old time rancher who, up in his 80s, was leasin his ranch out, puttin in his time. To say he was a little eccentric would be kind. He still drove and got around, but was kinda reckless. I had his ranch leased with a bunch steers on it, but we didn't live there. Our home was on the highway to Wickenburg. One day, when I got home, Mr. Rose's Cadillac was in the driveway. He was slumped over the wheel. Crap. I thought he cashed in. The front of the car was wrapped in barb wire and mesquite and grease wood stuck in the grill. I unloaded my horses and looked up, he was watchin me through the windshield. When I walked over to him, he smiled and asked if I could drive him home. The Caddy had a hole in the radiator and the engine was seized. Seemed he went to town for groceries and, on the way back, went to sleep, ran off the road, woke up, tromped on the gas pedal, and shot back onto the road at a different place in the fence!! That little deal cost a pretty penny, but he didn't seem to mind or quit drivin!!!!

Hide and Seek

We were gathering the west pasture for the spring works. This was one of the times the owner and his wife wanted to ride along. This pasture was big, rough, brushy, and miserable to gather. I loved it. We usually took three or four days to gather it. This was the last day and we were down to the roughest, rockiest, brushiest part where naturally the smartest, wildest, nastiest cows lived. All winter, I kept these cows scattered like a mad woman's chickens to make the water last and not gang the cows up in any one part.

I had the outside circle and was coming down a high ridge when the owner and his wife appeared below and about a quarter mile away. They were riding along at a slow snail's pace, smokin their Marlboros and not paying attention to anything in particular. I held up a minute so as not to get too far ahead of them as they needed watchin and would get lost. Soon, they split and rode on two sides of an oak thicket, still smokin and lookin down country and chatterin away. They were about a hundred feet past the thicket when a black white-face cow poked her head out of the thicket!!! She watched them ride away then very quietly turned up country, takin her big unbranded calf with her. Needless to say, I met that cow and calf a little while later after a hard ride cross country. When I got to the holdup, I had 10 pairs I had picked up behind them. The owners were surprised I had found them.

The New Vet

Anyone who knows me well will tell you I hate squeeze chutes. But it seems I have spent half my life standing next to one, processing cattle at one feed yard or another, then at ranches preg check in cows or wormin, or whatever. To quote an old friend, Leo Black, "the man who invented the squeeze chute didn't like to rope"!! Well, on this day the new vet was comin to vaccinate some replacement heifers. I had spent the day before oilin, replacin, and tighten up a rickey tickey off-brand chute. It had a guillotine head gate which meant you had to open one side of the chute with a cable-pulled lever. The boss NEVER took any interest in manual labor on the ranch, but today he shows up, new Bailey hat and new gloves. The vet shows up and I see why the boss is there. SHE is fresh outa vet school and fairly attractive in her form-fitting wranglers and tank top. We run the first heifer in and vaccinated and tagged her. The boss rushes by me to the controls on the chute and, without saying anything, pulls the cable that releases the side door!! With the heifer still squeezed, it slammed the gate open, knocking the vet 30 feet on to her wrangler-wrapped butt!!! The language that came out of that mouth!!! I looked up and the boss is hot-footin to his pickup with the vet yelling obscenities at his back. Never had to worry about him gettin in the way again!!!

Big Ole Button

This didn't happen to me, but it is such a good story I gotta tell it. The fella that started me into punchin cows was a big ole button from New Mexico who got a job on a big Arizona outfit packin grub to camps. In them days, everything was open, no fences, so lots of camps to keep cattle home. One camp set up an isolated canyon, real lonely and remote. Sam got into camp just at sundown, put his horse and pack string in the corral, and walked up to the tent the camp man used. He was sittin outside poundin jerky up for supper. He never knew Sam was within a hundred miles. Sam slipped up behind him real quiet, reached around and stole a piece of jerky. He still didn't see him. Sam stole another. Still didn't know he was there. Sam laid his hand in the skillet and left it there. Camp man looked down and damn near tore the tent down gettin away, ran a hundred yard before Sam tackled him!!!

Take Your Cows and Don't Come Back

Years ago, I had a ranch leased that was bordered on three sides by the Tohono O'odham Nation. I had to deal with four different grazing associations. Three were fine neighbors as good a people as I ever dealt with. I had the privilege of being the only white man to have permission to ride there. The fourth association was stand-offish and solemn, almost hostile.

Between the smugglers and Border Patrol cutting fences, it was a full-time job checking fences and keeping the cattle home. After a big summer rain, I was riding the south boundary checking water gaps. At an extra-large, deep wash the fence was gone and tracks going both ways. I fell into trackin them south hoping I would find them quick before those war-like boys from that fourth association found me. The farther I went the more trash I found; plastic, jugs, mason jars, etc. Just as I found the cattle, we stumbled into a clearing. A sweet smell was comin from a big copper kettle with a hot mesquite fire under it. Four big, hostile Indian men stood staring at me like I had three heads!!! One stepped up, looked at my cows, me, and said, "white man take your cows and don't come back"!!! His hand on a six-shooter!! In no time at all, all that was left of me there was the smell!!!!

I never said a word to anyone about that day, but that water gap had new wire the next day, and I didn't put it there!!!

My Rope is Still Rusty

Bob and I were helpin Art work his rough, rocky, central Arizona ranch. The only way you could work it was horseback, no vehicles, not even a four-wheeler. It was breakfast at 4, cooked on a wood stove, eaten by a kerosene lamp, leavin at a long trot an hour later, leanin out over the brow band. Many times, it was so dark you had to follow the sounds of the horse in front of you. The cattle weren't bad, but in country that rough, you always got some snotty ones. This one mornin, the wind was whistlin, cold and a hint of snow in the air, we were a good three hours from the house. We eased up on ledge that over looked a spring in a hole a quarter mile below, a good hour's ride. As we rested our saddle seats, on a trail below, a string of cattle came into view, single file, on the way to water. Art studied the cattle through his long eyes (binoculars) and pronounced the cattle as long-eared. "You boys stay here and catch what comes out, I'll go stir the pot with the dogs," he said. Art slipped off down the trail followed by five dogs. When he stirred the pot, those dogs kept the cattle circlin in that hole while Art caught and tied down one after another!!! Bob and I looked at each other like a couple fools. Presently, we saw a smoke down below. As we eased up to the fire, we counted nine head tied down. The last two were tied with rope cut off from Art's catch rope! "I guess I made a pig of myself," he says! "I guess so," Bob says, "my rope is still rusty"!!!

The Day Donnie Smiled

Years ago, I was helpin my friend gather his ranch to settle his divorce. When his wife left, he had set in the house and brooded for four years. Nothin got branded, nothin sold, just sat there. But now, the judge was forcin him to work his ranch. He had to sell enough to pay off his ex. She already had some of the patented land, now he had to give her cash. We had been gatherin for a week, findin cattle he never knew existed. His demeanor seemed to change as time went on, from gloomy to a little chipper, even makin a joke once in a while. Even though he was down in the dumps, I enjoyed workin for him. He was quiet and didn't like the crew being loud when workin. Everything went well, when one evening, we came into a brushy tank with a drive of 200 cows. We let them sift in, water, and sift out the other side. Donnie, the ranch owner, and I was holdin up the leaders when they come out the other side. When the drags came out into the open, there was the biggest crossbred steer I ever saw. His horns had been sawed off years ago and the brands had grown up into ridges on his sides. He belonged to the neighbors and he was rank as a boot full of snakes!! I had jerked down the twine and was ready for the wreck, but Donnie waved me off. I just pulled up and stared as that big sucker loped off up country. Damn, I was mad. Donnie never said another word until we were feedin the horses that night. That steer had gotten away for nine or ten years, and we didn't have time to fool with him.

Next mornin, as I was grainin the horses in the dark, Donnie eased up and said I needed to catch my best pony today, then went in to cook breakfast. When we went to saddle up, the boys from the next ranch were there. That was when Donnie told me that steer was back at that tank and we were goin after him. I had an old thoroughbred cross horse that I called Knife. He didn't care how rough it got or how far he had to run to catch the forked-toed critter!!

54

His only problem was he wouldn't pull your hat off your head! But he would hold anything ya caught.

When we got to the tank, it was just light enough to barely see. That old steer and a maverick cow were standin about 200 yard up country, right out in the open, big as life!! As we cinched up, the cattle left headed up country. Donnie and I made wild run but gottem stopped and turned down country. The cow split off and ole steer was rollin along like a Sunday freight train. When my loop went around his stub horns, it ran through his eyes and blinded him as long as I kept it tight. We goin downhill toward the trailers so, instead of stoppin him, I let him lope along as along as we went in the right direction. I knew if I ever stopped that steer, we were done. When we reached the trailer, I stopped ole Knife and let my dallies slip, turnin that steer around at the back of the open trailer. That steer was so strong he just started backin, takin my rope as he went. He just backed into the trailer clear to the front!! We tied him and he was in the Prescott sale barn by noon. He weighed 1975 almost twice what ole Knife weighed!! Donnie smiled that day!!

Hair-Raisin Stunts

I was helpin my friend and neighbor, Lyman, in the Santa Maria Mountains. He was up in years and needed some help movin cattle from pasture to pasture. His granddaughter Cathey was helpin, a skinny kid of 18 or 19. She worked at Old Tucson doin horses stunts and such. And, on top of that, she was a top hand at her age. Lyman's wife, Allaire, had cooked us a great lunch and we were sittin back enjoyin another glass of tea. Lyman ask me if I would shoe a horse for him before I left. Well, with a full belly I agreed to do it. I hadn't noticed Cathey had left the room. When I got to the barn to shoe the horse, there was Cathey with two broncs, and I mean broncs, tied together, ridin em roman inside that low roofed barn!! As she ducked rafters at a trot, she explained it was a stunt she had to do for a show later that month. Roman ridin in a barn and she was practicin! As the years went by, I watched her do some hair-raisin stunts with a horse. She had more guts than you can imagine!!!

The Snottiest and Rankest

We had been gatherin remnants off the 76 ranch for a few months and were gettin down to the snottiest and rankest that continually got away or who lived in inaccessible parts. My friend Wes had been helpin for about three days. With his dogs, and with mine, and Mrs. jefe, we had made a pretty good drag. In the corral, ready to load and go to town was a muley brangus bull who was on the fight and a horned crossbred cow about a hundred years old. She didn't seem too bad as long as she was with other gentler cows.

We cut the bull and three gentler cows into the loadin alley and run them up into the trailer for the ride to the sale barn. The bull and cows ran up the chute and jumped into the trailer like saddle horses. Without shutting any gates behind us, Wes and I jumped into the trailer to shut the divider gate. Before we could, here come the crossbred cow up behind us into the trailer!! A mad fightin bull on one end and a mad fightin cow on the other, inside a covered trailer!! For a minute it was hell amongst the yearlins!!!! The tailgate to the trailer was two piece that swung inside as well as out. Wes pulled half and I pulled half inside to cover us in the corners until those two old blisters went back down the alley!!! It took a little time to clean ourselves up and get back to loadin those cattle!!! And not all the crap was on the outside of our wranglers!!!!

Rockfish

In the not too distant past, Manuel and I were tracking some wild cattle in the Weaver Mountains. He was riding a blue roan Navaho pony called Rockfish. That horse was hard to shoe, unpredictable, and snaky to get on, but was a hell of a horse in rough country. The country was steep, rocky, and downright spooky in places. Manuel was in front, as he was the better tracker, when I saw him stop up ahead. The sign was gettin fresher and greener all the time. I expected to come up on the cattle any time. As I caught up to Manuel, I could see that he was lookin off the side of his horse, lost the trail. As I rode up, he turned in the saddle to speak to me. In front of him was a big smooth boulder five feet high and smooth as a bowling ball. Just as Manuel started to speak, rockfish jumped up on top of the boulder and balanced like an elephant on a beach ball!!!

Manuel started to shake and turned real slow and said, "ddddid yyyyou sssse tthat?" I nodded. Manuel slid off the right side and slid to the ground where his knees gave out. Rockfish hopped down and waited to regain the trail. It took Manuel a little longer!!!

Texans

In the early 70s, the International Feed Yard Team Roping Association had got off the ground. The first finals were held in Vegas at an outdoor arena on Thanksgiving weekend and was a frozen wreck. Hotel reservations were fouled up, the weather never got above 30 degrees. In spite of that, I was able to place in the mixed roping. Got a check and a new Resistal hat. Rex Allen did a concert in a big ole tent with about a hundred propane heaters tryin to keep our steaks warm while we ate them.

The next few years, the event was held in Elko, Nevada, at the Horse Palace indoor arena. It was still cold out, but we were all toasty inside!! The second year, I placed in the open roping, and the third year, I qualified with two partners in the open ropin. There were teams from Mexico, Canada, and Texas (that IS a foreign country, isn't it?). Anyway, one of my partners won the world with another Arizona roper and he and I placed third. Arizona ropers dominated the weekend. In order to get your check you had to go to a meeting where they were taking suggestions on how to improve the event. There were 20 Texans down front who were sayin we needed a cuttin or a calf ropin, maybe a team pennin. We said nothin because we just wanted our checks and wanted to leave. Presently, the man runnin the meeting asked what we Arizonans thought. My partner smiled and said he didn't care about a cuttin as we cut at home all day long at work. With that, a little smartass Texan stood up and said, maybe you Arizonans ain't got nothin will cut a cow. With that, partner smiled and said, "Maybe not, but we damn sure can rope, huh!!" With that, 20 Texans stood up and turned around!!! We got our checks and left!!!

Lookin for Cows

I was helping my friend Bud gather and ship his ranch. He had a hell of a string of steers scattered there north of Phoenix in Cave

Creek. The houses and ranchettes were taking the ranch over a little at a time and every pasture had a ton of houses, yards, and dogs runnin loose to contend with.

There was a Mexican cowboy in camp with us who was quite a character. He had ridden his own horse 20 miles to get a job there. He had a bed roll made up of a little Mexican serape and a big bottle of tequila.

The round up boss, Howard, was always laughin at Tony and tryin to set him up for a joke. We were workin a rough Malapi rock pasture one mornin, Howard was scatterin the riders as we made the back side circle. We came to a big, high, brushy, hog-back ridge with a stand of big trees on the top. Howard turned Tony off and told him to work the top of that ridge.

We had been at the holdup about an hour when Tony came in with a little bunch of steers. He was awful quiet, which wasn't Tony. Finally, Howard couldn't stand it anymore. "What did ya see, Tony," he asked. Tony looked around at us and smiled, "Lots of peoples there no gotta any ropas (clothes). I told this naked lady, 'I'm lookin for cows, lady, not chee-chees!!'" It took a while for us to get back to work!!

Swearing to Buddha

I had been hired sight unseen by a couple of California steer speculators who were planning on stocking Arizona with 20 thousand steers in the winter. We had moved our family almost overnight from Wickenburg to Picacho, Arizona to start receiving steers on the first of three ranches they had leased. All arrangements had been made by these guys' banker. After three weeks, I still hadn't met these guys and they had handed me a checkbook and expense money. I had been told to pay myself what I thought was fair!!! They had instructed me to get a cell phone, one of the first I had. It was a bag phone that lived in my pickup and had a real scratchy quality.

One afternoon, as I was waitin on trucks to bring more steers, this bag phone went off. When I answered, it was one of my bosses I had never met. "Is there a landing strip nearby?" he asked. I told him where one was and drove there to meet him. It was a short strip used by crop dusters and had power lines on one end. Soon, a tri-cycle

Beechcraft roared over at treetop height, circled, and came in over the power lines!! When he set it down, the tail feathers had to brush those power lines!! He touched down on one wheel, skeed along on the one tire, then set down on all three wheels, skittered down the strip, did a U-turn in front of my pickup, and settled like a spastic hen on a prickly pear nest!! The prop hadn't even stopped turnin when the side door flew open and a very attractive brunette fell out on hands and knees spittin four letter words and callin my boss names that I hadn't ever heard!! I could hear him laughin while she was swearin to Buddha that she would NEVER get in another airplane with him again!!

Tropical Swamp Angels

After the boss had looked at all the Mexican steers we could find in the pickup and the brunette had cooled off, we stopped at a little roadside tavern and ordered Coronas and lime. The boss laid a new one on me: he was sendin me a bunch of Hawaiian heifers. OK, I had had a dose of Floridian cattle and the first thing envisioned was more of those tropical swamp angels and I said so. But the boss assured me they weren't nothin like Florida gater bait. No brahma, all English breeding and, yes, they were trotty because Hawaiian cowboys don't do nothin at a walk, but these cattle will get gentle with the right work.

It seems that the 50th state overproduces beef and, with a closed economy, can't consume them fast enough, so they export them to the mainland. These cattle will acclimate to Arizona real well. And the ones I got did, gaining almost four pounds a day on good afilaree. And, yes, they were trotty. REAL trotty.

When time to ship these BIG fat heifers with remnants of grass skirts, the boss impressed on me not to spend a lot of money on shippin corrals (this pasture had NONE!!) and to make it so we could pick it up and take it with us when done. Me and two Latin American boys built a water lot, crowding alley, and sortin pens outta T-Posts and net wire!!! With a portable loadin chute, we were in business!! When we had the corral full of cattle, we would park our pickups and trailers along the fence on the outside to keep the cattle from crowding that net wire!! When a semi got there, we would sort off a load and load the truck as we sorted, never spilled a drop in three days work, but that net wire corral was gettin pretty ragged!!! The second day was the only day we came close to a wreck. The boss was on one end of the alley sortin off a truck load. I was watchin the gate behind him. The brunette and my wife were loadin the alley. With the alley loaded, the brunette, who was wilder than an outhouse mouse, over-undered her horse and hollered at the boss she was comin to help him!!! That brown pony went hurtlin up the middle of the alley full of cattle with the boss wavin his hands and hollerin to stop. When she got up to him, not one heifer had jumped nor hit that wire fence!!! The boss, me, and my Mrs. let out a long breath as the boss looked at me smiled and said gggggggooooood fence!!!

Let a Cowboy Do It

When I took over the 76 ranch, we found there was a lot of ungathered remnants... and then we found out WHY!! I have never, in my life, dealt with a more sour, spoilt bunch of good quality cows in my life. Fortunately, the boss had bought that great historic ranch with the brand. Me and the Mrs. found out real quick these cattle would run until they fell over dead before they would allow you to hold them up. Some did!! There was a couple bulls who would, when reaching a certain point in the pasture, just simply turn back over whoever was trying to hold them up. If you roped one, the Budweiser hitch couldn't move them!! They had been roped and turned loose so many times there was no leading them. One bull, no matter where you were, would hide in the brush then attack and turn your horse over if he could. If he couldn't, he would give chase, hookin your horse in the butt for as long as a quarter mile!!! The one thing those cows respected was dogs, they had been worked with heelers and when a dog came around, they stopped to fight, knowing those dogs would chew on their heels or the calves. It was easy work for a bunch of young Catahoula catch dogs. Within a few months, we had thinned that bunch down to a handful of the oldest and worst. Whenever we got a gooseneck load gathered, they went to the sale barn. Our only day off came on sale day. Being a stranger in this country, I didn't know a lot of folks, so one day, at the sale, a package of those old renegades came in the ring. The previous owner, who was now livin in a rest home, was sittin down front with his son-in-law. The son-in-law leaned over and told the old man, "See. They're stealin your cows!" The old man looked at the son-in-law and smiled and said, "I bought that ranch that way I guess I can sell it that way! 'Sides you had your chance and couldn't get 'em. Let a cowboy do it!!!"

Ned and Wiley

When at the 76 ranch, I had the best dogs I ever had, Catahoula-Border Collie crosses. The leaders were litter mates, Ned and Wiley. No matter what you did, Ned was always out front of your horse with his nose in the air checkin the breeze for cow smell. Wiley stayed behind your horse, unless Ned left on a scent. Man, it was fun to watch'em work. One spring mornin, I was workin my way down a rocky trail on the way to meet the Mrs. at a wind mill down below me, a mile or so away. All of a sudden, I heard Wiley yelp. I looked back and he was sittin there holdin one foot up with two drops of blood on the top of it. A BIG rattle snake was slowly crawlin into the rocks. The bugger never made a sound as I rode by, but hit Wiley as he came along. It was early enough in the spring that the mornins were cool, almost cold. I reached down and grabbed him by the scruff of the neck and struck a lope to that wind mill down below with Wiley in my lap. The Mrs. saw me comin and knew somethin was wrong. When I got to the mill, the water there was still cold from the night chillin. I sat Wiley down in the trough to chill. After a minute or so, he stiffened and I was afraid I was too late, but he came back around. Then when he seemed better, I grabbed him and hit a lope to the next mill where the truck was. Again, I put him that cool water for a few minutes. The Mrs. loaded the horses and started the truck. We threw Wiley in the cab (no dog was allowed there) and started the 30 mile trip to the vet. As we went by the house, we grabbed a sack of ice and took off again with Wiley's foot packed in ice. At the vet, she gave him two vials of anti-venom, then said not to expect much. Two days later the vet called and said to come get him!!! No ill effects or infection and Wiley was back to work in two more days. Both Ned and Wiley are gone now. I don't think they would like not havin cattle to work, so I guess it's best, but I still miss seein those two hold up a bunch of trotty old nellies!!

Johnny Long

The story I'll tell you today is one time, in about twenty, that I was involved in with the same scenario. I have never known this set of circumstances to go well, but for some reason cattle owners continue to try it.

I was at the Rafter Six ranch in the mid-70s, one of three ranches the boss owned. He also had a feedlot. One of these three ranches was the battle Ax, one rough, cholla infested booger. The Gila River ran live on the southern border for 12 miles. 12 miles of thickets and not so much as a suggestion of fence or other kind of boundary. In the middle of the ranch stood a mesa with one trail up and down, little to no water on top. Every trail on the ranch was enclosed in cholla thickets. Rocks, cholla, and mountain lions, a real wonderful place.

One night the boss called to say he had two truckloads of brangus heifers he wanted to put on the back side of Bronco Mesa at a windmill called Johnny Long. The heifers had been in the feed lot 60 days, warmin up. Me and a couple other punchers were to wait at the Battle Ax corrals, which set on a solid rock nob in sight of the highway, with my wife's little brother along. He was 14 at the time and never worked cattle in his life, let alone in this kind of country. When the trucks unloaded, it was plain to see these were farm cattle with no knowledge of open country or cholla. When we opened the gates, it was a quarter mile to the first cholla patch. There, the cattle had to narrow down to two or three abreast, didn't happen. They hit the cholla and stampeded, each animal picking up cholla, runnin to their buddy and stickin them, it spread like a chain reaction. The cattle runnin every which way, lookin like black pin cushions with all that cholla stickin all over them. The farther they ran, the worse it got. There was no way in gods heaven to hold them up. And then it snowed! In the next hour it snowed, it rained, and the cattle were no closer to Johnny Long than I was to heaven. At one little narrow place, I looked around for my brother-in-law and he wasn't there. Asking one of the other boys, they pointed down a rocky draw a mountain goat wouldn't go down, comin out of was Bo and five heifers; him, horse, and cattle covered in cholla, but still upright. About dark, we got back to headquarters after gettin about two thirds of those flat land cattle to the mill. The rest were scattered like a mad woman's chickens. I heard, years later, that some of those grown up heifers still ran there ungathered. And would you believe it, I almost leased that ranch for the wild cattle there. Thank god the Mrs. talked me out of it.

Aqui

When I was at the Rafter Six Ranch in Kearny, I had 250 acres of permanent pasture to irrigate. So, every mornin I would go out set the water so it would run on a 12 hour set, then do my ranch thing until about 5 in the afternoon. Then, I would set the night water to run until daylight the next mornin. I had a Mexican cowboy who was stayin there and, every evening, he would take my year old son and teach him Spanish. The big word was aqui, "here" in English. One night, I went to change the water just a sundown. I took Ty along.

While I was changing the water, I left Ty in the pickup for fear of him gettin on a snake. When I went to leave we had no keys!! When I would ask Ty, he would say aqui and point out the window. The grass was almost knee-high. I looked and searched but found no keys. All the time Ty is sayin aqui and pointing out the window. Finally, I put Ty on my shoulders and started walkin home, two miles away. Man, was I mad. But I knew it was my own fault for leavin the keys in the truck. When I got home I called a friend of mine who was a good mechanic to come put a new ignition set in the truck. Next mornin, I saddled a pony and trotted down to change the water. After I had, I stepped into the stirrup and, as I did, I looked down on the bed of the truck. In the bed is a hole right behind the cab and in that hole was... you guessed it... key!!!!!!

Buckeroos

Years ago, I had a ranch leased in Aguila, Az. It had one big pasture of 45 sections that was bordered by a great big, ugly mountain on the north and a real fence on the south. I had turned out 500 head of steers for a farmer who wanted to be a steer man. When it came time to gather and ship, this farmer hired two couples of buckeroos and sent them to me for help. They had a good camp outfit and 8 head of big ole horses that, anywhere else, would make their livin pullin a wagon full of tourists. Every mornin these buckeroos would "rope those poor ole ponies when a moral with a teaspoon full of grain would catch them all. First mornin, they all turned out with Bermuda chaps (chinks).

When I tried to suggest they may want some chaps, they made it clear they used these chinks everywhere they went. There was a pipeline that ran the length of this pasture, right down the middle, with a drinker about every mile and a half. As we left the corrals, I noticed my wife's horse had a little bob to his head, so I took it kinda easy until we reached the end of the pipeline. All the way there, I could hear them buckeroos talkin about our little desert ponies. This was late May and it was gonna get hot, and soon, but this bunch of meadow hay balers had no idea what they were into. When I reached the end of the pipeline, I turned my wife around and told her to take her time and just work the pipeline and take care of her pony. The road ended there and it was a good four miles to the back fence. As we left the last tub and my wife, I kicked into a long trot. The temperature was already in the 90s. As I passed these buckeroos, I told them it was time to go and, if they were goin with me, to come on. When we reached the back side, those big ole half perchon horses were heavin and drippin sweat.

I scattered them out kinda thin and took the outside circle. When we got back to the corrals, my wife was waitin in the shade and about 100 head of steers in the corral, full and layin down. I added 20 or so and the four buckeroos got in with 5 between them. They also reported seein more but couldn't get them because of the cactus!! These poor pilgrims were good, likable people, but like most buckeroos couldn't, or wouldn't, adjust to the ways of a different country. Before we got through, they had figured out that cattle can walk, that chaps do work, and every horse doesn't need ropin, those 1000 pound ponies we rode could get around the rough country and cactus. Those monsters they rode couldn't.

Hula Hoop

When I worked for the Forepaugh Cattle Co., in Aguila, I got to do a lot of things and I saw a lot of things. Most made me scratch my head. Forepaugh was 250 sections of pretty good desert country. It was almost all deeded and state grazing leases, but as my memory serves me, the pasture called Summer Camp was BLM. Just those three letters tell all anyone needs to know about it. Federal agencies are NEVER good. Some individuals who work there are good, honest people with some common sense, but most can't pour piss out of a boot. At the Forepaugh, they ran around four hundred mother cows and, if it rained, turned out bunches of steers to take advantage of the feed. The Summer Camp was used for those mother cows and it was a seasonal deal. It could have run a lot more year round, but the range conservationist put a stop to that. We never could get them to tell us how they arrived at the numbers they would allow there.

One day, I was back there prowlin and checkin those cows when I saw a strange thing. There was a guy with a sun helmet (like you'd see in a Tarzan movie), shorts, a tee shirt with a rock and roll band painted on it, and brogan boots with high white socks. He had sunglasses and a clip board with some kind of preprinted form on it. He also had a hula hoop. Now, we were thirty miles from town and on a two-track dirt road and this cat is playin with a hula hoop!! His truck was parked back in the brush and could barely be seen. He hadn't seen me yet, so I just sat my horse to see what this clown was gonna do. He was writin on the clipboard when I rode up, head down studyin that piece of paper. Then all of a sudden, he up and throws that hula hoop. It landed on an ant hill about a hundred feet away. He marches over to it, gets down on his prayer bones, and starts countin!!! 1, 2, 3, and so on. I figure he's countin ants!! But pretty soon, somethin told him someone was watchin him. He looks around and sees me. Waves and says hi, comes marchin over with his hand outstretched. Out of reflex, I reach to shake when I see he has a business card in his hand!! OK, I take it and it says he's a range con outta Phoenix. OK, I says, nice to meet ya, what ya doin. Countin grass, he says. Throw the hoop then count the plants in the hoop and that tells them how many cows we can run here!! But it landed on an ant hill, I says!!! No grass there, why not over there where the grass is solid and thick? Oh, that wouldn't be fair, he says!! A week later we got a letter cuttin the permit in half!!!! Now, THAT ain't fair!!!!

Snake!!!

Now, anyone who knows me knows that I cannot stand the touch of a reptile, any reptile!!! Frogs, lizards, horn toads, snakes, can't stand it!!! When little, my kids got great pleasure in chasing me around with a frog!!

While at the Forepaugh ranch, the boss there had a routine that didn't vary a minute every day. About 4 o'clock, Russ would get a six pack and take off for the Summer Camp well. He took enough gas to run the pump long enough until the next day at the same time again. The road there was narrow, slow and kinda rough, so Russ would idle along, sip beer there and back, except for the snakes. When he saw a rattle snake he stopped, took out his trusty shovel and dispatched Mr. snake, then load him in the back of the truck for a prank back home. I had gotten like a locoed horse around the barn and corrals. Russ was always settin a dead snake where it would scare me.

This one summer afternoon, I had been shoein horses and it got kinda late. It was just dark enough that you could still make out a person, but not a lot else. Russ was parked on the road I had to take home, visiting with another driver when I pulled up. My kids and wife were with me and elected to stay in the truck while I got out to see Russ. Now, I knew that meant drinkin a beer and getting a report on the water situation at Summer Camp. As I walked up, Russ swung his arm in a wide arc and I saw something leave his hand, something long and round, then it hit me across the chest.... a snake.

The rattles still on, it rattled as it hit the ground at my feet. I was froze, couldn't move. Russ eased up, picked up the dead snake, and handed me a cold beer. I told him if I could move I would choke him. That snake had spattered blood all across my shirt and face!! To this day I can smell that blood. My kids are still laughin!!!

Burro Creek

Times were tough. We had a roof over our heads, but no work. One afternoon, our friend Lyman stopped at the house to ask for some help. It seems he had been to the hospital in Prescott to visit a friend when he met some folks who had the old Loving U Ranch in the bottom of Burro Creek outside of Bagdad. Well, Lyman knew no strangers, and struck up a conversation with these folks. It seems they had a problem, about 20 to be exact, all running freely in Burro Creek!! Now, Burro Creek run live water year round here and the BLM was real worried that 20 head of cattle would destroy the fragile environment along that creek bottom. They were demanding the cattle be removed at once. Well, it seems the owners were nice folks with great educations, but absolutely no knowledge of gathering the forked-toe, rock-hoppin cow brute. Well, the upshot was Lyman contracted the gather on these cattle, but he needed help and he knew I needed work, so a deal was made. A few days later we pulled up to the edge of Burro Creek. What a sight!! The road snaked down to the bottom at about an 8 percent grade over rock and clay. We unhooked our trailers on the top, one man leading our horses and Lyman and myself driving and sliding our trucks down to the corrals and camping spot.

After setting up camp, staking the dogs (Lyman brought four), and eating a good supper, we went to bed in preparation for the next day's gather. Three men, four dogs, and six horses after 20 head in a canyon no wider than a half mile at the widest, piece of cake!!!

Next day we made a good drag and got 18 head with the dogs doin the dirty work. We penned these cattle and were tickled with our good work. When the owner showed up that night with a Bobtail truck to haul the cattle, he mentioned that he neglected to tell us there were two young bulls that also needed gathering. That made a grand total of 4 head. Tomorrow they would be in the corral, we bragged. Good cowboys, good horses, good dogs; what else could be the outcome. That night, things took a downhill turn. The dogs got loose and got into the chuck box. Next mornin, we found, though not completely wiped out, we were short on grub. About ten that mornin, we jumped the two cows who were amongst the missing. Both had month old calves and were in no mind to go to the corrals. They split with one pair headed toward the corrals and the other down canyon. It took the whole crew to pen that one old Herford cow and calf. Somewhere in the wreck I spilt the last of my snuff and, when I went to the chuck box, I found the dogs had scattered my stash!! In those days, being without Copenhagen was the same as being insane!!! After a night of no nicotine and no coffee at breakfast (the dogs ruined that too), we set out after the remaining cattle. We decided that win, lose, or draw, we were outta there that night.

Sure enough, we jumped the cow and calf and, as they made a dash for the brush, I caught that ole nellie right around the horns. While tying her to a tree, our third hand, Marty, came busting out of the brush in hot pursuit of the two bulls. There was a water gap fence about a hundred yards away with a narrow gate in it. That gate was open. Just as the first bull went through the gate, Marty roped him with a rope tied to the saddle horn. That bull jerked Marty's horse sideways into the gate, thus plugging it. The second bull was trotting along the fence looking for a hole when we got there. At sight of us, that bull ran up to a point of ground overlooking a big pool of water. There, the bull turned to fight. The dogs took to the bull who then turned and dived into the pool with a dog on each ear. All three disappeared under water!!! I was about to follow and, right then, decided it wasn't Saturday!! When the bull surfaced, there was a dog on each side and again they took to the bull. When they came out of the water, I was waitin and caught the bull, tying him to a gentle cotton wood tree. By now I was gettin pretty ringy with no Copenhagen!! Marty and Lyman were kinda stayin away and didn't have a lot to say. We necked those bulls together, blindfolded them, and they drove to the corrals. Along the way, I picked up the cow and led them in, all the while gettin crankier and crankier!! When we loaded out, Marty, without a word, grabbed the horses and started up the road while Lyman and I spun our tires all the way to the top of the canyon. Hooked up, loaded, and rollin, we made Bagdad in about two hours over rough road. Lyman pulled over and went into the Quik Stop, coming back with a cold beer for each of us and a bonus for me, a can of Copenhagen!! Nothin was better!! A couple hours later, I was home with a check, a fresh can of snuff, and a smile on my face!

Tyson

I had a friend who lived in the artillery peaks, with his wife, on a ranch she inherited. It had been in her family three or four generations. It was a great place! One road into the house, no others. If you got around, it was horseback. The old pack trail from Wickenburg to the mining town of Sentenal ran through there in solid rock. That trail was wore a foot deep and just wide enough for a mule or horse. My friend, Art, worked that ranch with his wife and sister-in-law, very seldom hiring help. I got to go help a few times. It was a treat. His wife, Patsey, cooked on a wood stove, and I mean it was good. The water came from a spring, into the house in a half inch pipe through the wall, and ended with a faucet over a bucket with a dipper in it. The bunk house was down in the creek bottom and was spotless. Lanterns were the illumination of choice although there were a few kerosene lamps in the main house. Heat was a fire place and the cook stove. The house was adobe so in the summer, if you left the windows open, it was always cool. Art used a lot of dogs, catch dogs, as a lot of Art's cattle were a little tough to hold up by yourself. His main dog, at that time, was a big red merled dog he called Tyson. He was named after a friend's son.

This one day we were out lookin for an old wild cow that Art was wanting to ship to the sale. We had rode for hours, hoppin from pinnacle to pinnacle, prowlin the highest most inaccessible areas of the ranch. Finally, Art pulled up and got down on a rock with his binoculars. After about ten minutes, he quietly said there she is. After following his finger, pointing across the canyon, I could make out a red spot on a ledge.

After riding for another a hour, we came up on the ledge. It was about ten feet wide and maybe sixty long. This shelly old cow was laying on the far end, drooling, her eyes sunk in her skull. This cow would never make the trip to the house, let alone to Phoenix. She was done. She heaved to her feet and immediately went on the fight. Before anyone could say anything, Tyson boiled by and grabbed this old nellie by the nose. Tyson weighed a good 100 pounds; that old poor cow probably 700. As Tyson sat back to hold the cow, she started walking backwards. She was draggin the dog and bawlin at the same time. The dog was settin back for all he was worth. Art shook his head and, just above a whisper, called Tyson's name. The dog simply opened his mouth. That old cow fell over backwards, over the cliff, killed her, graveyard dead. Art sat there, rolled a cigarette and then turned his horse back to the house. "Chalk up one for Tyson," was all he said.

Ole Dave

I was workin for Dave down at Alamo Lake. He had about a thousand steers turned out on the desert there. Alamo Lake was fenced off up to what was called Three Rivers at Brown's Crossing. The big Sandy and the Santa Maria come together to form the Bill Williams River that flows a whole three miles into the lake. Brown's Crossing was where the rivers came together there. All that was left was giant ole dead cotton wood trees. Dave's steers weren't supposed to be around the lake or in the Three Rivers area.

One night, the park ranger came to the ranch to tell us that some fisherman had left the gate open and a bunch of steers had gotten into Three Rivers. There was a gal camping there, watching some bald eagles that were nesting in the dead cottonwoods. She was afraid that one of the eagles would fall out of the nest and the steers would step on it. Dave assured her that the eagles wouldn't hurt the steers, but she failed to see the humor. Dave told them we would be there the next mornin at daylight to get the steers. What no one knew was: Dave had opened that gate. The waters were drying up on the desert and those steers needed to drink at the lake and river. Of course, the enviros and fishermen couldn't stand that, cow crap in the water and pee on the trails!!!

Next mornin, five of us unloaded our horses on the bluff overlookin Brown's Crossing, and sure enough, those steers were bedded around the old cottonwoods. Now, the river here is notorious for quicksand. Not like you see in the movies, but it will bog a horse or cow, sometimes really deep. When we all cinched up, Dave said in a whisper that sounded as loud as a bull horn, you all wait here I'll find us a crossing. He rode down to the river bank, rode up and down a three times for effect the turned and said we can cross here, be quiet!! With that, he rode ole Punkin into the river and bogged him to the saddle skirts!!!! "@#$@#$" Dave yelled as old Punkin rolled over on him mashing down into the sand and water!!! When Dave yelled, those steers left there like the hounds of hell were in pursuit!! Bob went by Dave on one side, me on the other, at a dead run. Dave was cussin and diggin sand and mud out from under his glasses and hat, leading a waterlogged Punkin back to dry land. Those steers tore the river bottom up leavin there. There was no way to turn them, so Bob and I went back up the bluff. As we got there, the ranger was sayin:

70

see Annie, ole Dave put those steers right where he wanted them!! Bob looked at me and said: a dunkin in the river was a cheap price for waterin those steers!!!

Horse Tracks and a Runnin Iron

Ya know, for my whole life, small ranchers and town ranchers have been suspicious of a man who gets up before daylight and is five miles along when the sun comes up, lookin out over the brow band. I guess it's just they think: if you're not sittin there in the coffee shop with them, there's somethin wrong with you!! Those people, who think that coffee shop won't get along without their business, just seem to be more important than the rest of us!! The few times I spent time in those coffee shops, it seems those people knew more about everyone else's business than the folks they were talkin about!!

Then ya got brand inspecters. They are a valuable asset to the cowman except for their own image of self-importance!! Pin a badge on one and, by god, anyone and everyone is a suspect!! And as they move around the country inspecting brands, they spread their gossip like a fertilizer spreader!! So while you're out makin horse tracks and mindin your business, the coffee shop stool polishers are goin at ya with forked tongues!!

Years ago, I went to the 76 ranch. There, I found years of poor management had left a mess for the new owner. A remnant that was spoiled, corrals run down, water wells that wouldn't pump, tanks that hadn't been cleaned in years. Now, in my limited experience, I've found the only way to correct these problems was to pull your hat down and go to work!! My neighbor on the east was an old puncher who was puttin his last years takin care of a little ranch for an absentee owner. Ole Bill had been up the river and over the mountain. He was a hand!!

The neighbor on the west was a big, loudmouthed ex-football player who had owned a dozen ranches and never stayed on one long enough to find his way to the horse corral. HE spent his time at the coffee shop, or the USDA office tryin to find free government money. His cows never seemed to produce enough calves, but, then, with old bulls and not enough bulls, what do you expect.

Thursday was sale day and a lot of ranchers went to town for the sale. Old Bill was there one day, after unloadin his calves, havin coffee in the cafe at the sale barn. The bigmouth football player was sittin there with him. Old Bill ask him how he could spend all his time in town knowing his neighbor was ridin every day, carrin a runnin iron, and with 10 miles of bad fence between the two ranches? The football player spewed his coffee out and got up and stormed out of the cafe, Old Bill was laughin himself silly until he realized he got stuck with the check!!!

Peaches

Why is it, when you're runnin a ranch for a dude, they want to bring all their town friends to help? Most of them are nice people, well intentioned, but basically they get in the way. When I was younger, I had no time for those folks. Maybe that was why I didn't stay anywhere too long. As I got older, I became more tolerant of those folks. They can't help it if they didn't have the education we did. I mean, they spent all their time bein lawyers, doctors, and such, while we learned a more important trade: feedin the country. But we had dirt under our fingernails and so....

Anyway, we were brandin at the 76. We were shorthanded and so I was kinda puttin up with a couple of town dogs who were there at the invite of the owners. I can honestly say they were better help than the owners. As the day progressed, we got into the swing of things and were gettin things done. One of these town dogs was a little uppity, but not bad, so when we stopped for lunch, I kinda watched him turn his nose up at the bill of fare, but he did get a plate and nibble at the lunch my wife made for the crew, who was chowing down. We had an ice chest with cold drinks and cans of fruit for dessert.

I had a can of peaches and was sittin on the edge of the water trough spearin peaches out of the can with my knife when this persnickety feller asked if that was the same knife I used all day castrating bulls and ear marking calves. I nodded and rolled a peach to the other side of my mouth and said, "yeah, but..." Hell, he was already pukin down on his hands and knees!! I was gonna tell him I washed it first, but changed my mind.

Dave Roped a Lion.

I wasn't along when this happened, but I was close and this is the way Dave told it to me:

Dave and Liz was on the way in to the house after dark one night, the moon was the only light. Dave always rode with his rope tied hard and fast, with a loop in his hand that he slapped his chap leg with as he rode. They were followin a trail in the Santa Maria River bottom that wound through a cottonwood sapling thicket. Dave said it had been a tough day, a long day, and he was anxious to get home. Just as he came around a bend in the thicket, a dark form jumped out in front of him. Out of reflexes, Dave threw that loop at the scurrying form and the rope drew up tight on a lion!! Now a roped lion has to be one of the most animated things alive!! Liz told me later that lion tore up half the cottonwood saplings in the river bottom. Finally, Mr. lion wrapped himself up in a big tree. All this time Dave had his hands full keeping his horse from stampeding down the river!! When the lion got wrapped up good enough to get near, Liz got of her horse and clubbed the lion so Dave could get loose.

Next day, after skinnin the lion, Dave took off for Wickenburg. He headed straight to the La Cabana bar where he held forth all day long on his favorite bar stool telling anyone who would listen how he roped a lion!! Now not just anyone can rope a lion, so Dave was pretty proud.

Two days later at the ranch, a convoy of trucks and cars wound their way down the road to the ranch. Fish and Game, park ranger, county deputies, and a BLM agent. When Dave met them in the yard, they arrested him and Liz for killin the lion without a two dollar lion tag!! Before the deal was over, they had to pay over 1200 dollars in fines, each, and didn't even get to keep the hide!! But Dave said it was worth it so he could tell everyone how he roped a lion!! I don't think Liz was as enthused!!!

Pay Attention!!

At the 76 ranch, we turned the weaned calves back out to grow into yearlins, trying to make 600 pounders out of them. We were under-stocked, so we almost always had extra feed for them. I saved one pasture just for those calves, so it was always good. Now the owner didn't like to leave the house. He wasn't overly ambitious as far as anything physical was concerned, but he took a likin to Mrs. jefe's cookin and started showin up to ride when we gathered cows or yearlins. Of course, then he would have to ride and work with us, and because he was the owner, he didn't try to give orders or be bossy. He was good that way. I kept his horse shod and ready whenever I thought he wanted to go, which wasn't very often.

This particular fall, the yearlins had done extra good. The summer rains had put a lot of water in the tanks and the gramma grass was stirrup-high, and the summer mesquite bean crop had been heavy so those black baldie yearlins, instead of weighing 600, were closer to 700 pounds!! I consigned two truckloads to a special stocker sale in November. I knew these big black baldies would knock a hole in the market. I ordered trucks for the Wednesday before the sale, then called my friend, Wes, to come help gather Monday and Tuesday then help load out on Wednesday. When Wes got to the ranch on Monday mornin, the owner followed him through the gate. Mrs. jefe had breakfast ready and the boss wasn't gonna miss it. The pasture was about 15 sections, flat, with a southern drainage. The draws were heavy with mesquite. There was a well-traveled dirt road that split the pasture east to west. The north half wasn't as heavy with the brush as the south half. We worked the south half first, throwin all the cattle north of the road into a dirt tank where we held them to settle them and water out. You could see a long ways into the north and one man could cover a big piece of country alone, so I sent Wes up north and we started the drive down the road to the shippin pens. I made it real plain to everyone NOT to let those yearlins south of the road or we would lose them in those thickets. The first two miles went well.

Mrs. jefe took the drags; the owner the swing; and I had the point. As we topped a rise, I noticed Wes was about a mile above us trying to turn a bunch of cattle to the drive and not havin much luck. The drive was strung out good, walkin along like milk cows headed to the distant corrals. I hollered at the boss and told him to keep the cattle like they were and I would go help Wes. He nodded as if he understood. I loped off in Wes's direction. Sure enough, that bunch was hard to turn, but between the two of us we turned them to the corrals. There was a lane that led into the corrals about a mile long.

Our bunch got there just as the leaders from the main drive hit the gate, easy sailin from there on. One thing puzzled me was Mrs. jefe was in the lead and the owner was on the drags. That night, when everyone went home, I asked the Mrs. what had happened to cause her to switch with the owner.

She explained I had no more than gotten out of sight when those yearlins started crossin the road into a thicket on the south side. The owner was smokin his Marlboro, lookin at the clouds, and lettin the cattle scatter. She quit her post, made a run up through a thicket and turned the cattle back to where they belonged. That was when she told the owner to pay attention or no more biscuits for breakfast!! He told me later that she went by him like a pay wagon passin a tramp and told him to put the damn cigarette away and pay attention!!

Donkey Catchers

Many years ago, a wise bureaucrat decided there was entirely too many donkeys in the Grand Canyon. He convinced the higher ups to fund an expedition to gather those donkeys and relocate them to Alamo Lake. Now I don't know if ANYBODY knew how many donkeys were in the canyon, but a certain enterprising puncher decided there was plenty. And if there wasn't, he would make sure there was!!

Sure enough, that puncher got the contract to gather those little fellers that had just wreaked havoc on the environment of the 7th Wonder of the World. He convinced the Feds they needed a chopper to spot the burros and about five men to give chase and rope them. Then he needed an extensive set of panel corrals and a truckload of hay to hold and feed the donkeys until he shipped them to Alamo Lake. In the mornin, they would ship a bobtail load out and, at Alamo Lake, there was a Fed who unloaded and counted the little fellers. But, what nobody knew was, there was a second crew of cowboys at the lake that would re-gather the donkeys, load em up, and haul them back to the canyon at night and release them!! Why, before it was over, some of those donkeys, when roped, would just turn and run to a truck and jump in and wait for the ride!! The upshot was that puncher whose idea it was to rope and gather those donkeys made enough on the deal to buy a pretty good little ranch!!! Thanks to the Fed!!

Suzy the Dog

When I was a button, five years or so, my dad took a job at a ranch that was up on the Agua Fria River. The camp we had was old, and isolated, just a few yards from the river. I remember that old house as being adobe with big high ceilings. When we moved there, there was an old yellow dog laying on the screen porch. She came to us waggin her tail and lookin for a pet. There was a note on the door that said the dog's name was Suzy and it would be best to keep her there as she warned of snakes. Now, I don't remember all this, but my Mom told this many times. Suzy became my best friend and companion. When I went with Dad to milk the cow, Suzy was always in front on that rocky trail to the corral. Many a time she would point out a snake by the trail. She would circle the snake, barking and howling, until Dad got there to deal with Mr. snake. There was a barbwire fence along the road and I remember Dad hanging those snakes he killed on that fence; more than anyone can remember.

Many times, at night, we would wake to Suzy barking and caring on out in the yard. Dad would get up and kill the snake then we would go back to bed. She would even point out scorpions and centipedes crawling up the walls. I don't remember the exact amount of time we lived there, but I know Mom was about to pull her hair out over the snakes. I started school there in a one-room school and rode a little yellow bus to a back. Me and a little blonde-haired girl were the only ones in the first grade. We even had a Christmas play. I remember that.

Dad found another job, back in Maricopa, where he stayed the rest of his life. But we always remember Suzy, who we left there for the next folks to come along. I was worried about her getting to eat, but dad said the ranch owners cared for her. Not many folks get friends like her.

Baggy Pants and a Rattlesnake

A few years ago, we moved to Bowie where we bought an old cotton farm. We weren't gonna farm cotton, but it had good fences around it, a nice house, and barn. We could keep a few cattle, our horses and be comfortable. But as with all old farms it had a scrap pile of junk equipment, pieces of wore out farm implements, and scrap metal. A big junk pile. Well, after we got settled, I set about cleanin up the mess. After a day or so I realized it was a greater chore than I imagined. After making a few phone calls, I hit upon a plan that would clean up the mess and make a few bucks in the process.

I contacted a scrap recycler in Tucson who was willing to bring a semi-trailer and park it at our place. All I had to do was load it and they would haul it away and send me a check!! Can't beat that.

As I got started with the little chore, I realized that there had to be a nest of rattlesnakes somewhere about. I killed about a dozen in the first week. After a couple weeks of steady work, I had that trailer loaded and could see that I had about another load or two yet.

They brought me an empty trailer and picked up the full one and I was back in business. I had a little ranch leased nearby, so I had to take time to look after it. Between that and loading the second trailer, it took me a little longer to get it loaded, but load it I did. I called the scrapyard to come pick it up. They told me their truck was broke down, but would send a contract trucker.

When this contract truck arrived, it was driven by a young fellow who was pleasant enough, even though his britches were half off his butt and draggin the ground. I showed him how to get to the trailer and, while he went to hook up, I went back to shoeing a horse. Presently, I looked up and this kid was runnin every which way, wavin his arms, and I could hear a faint shriek from him. I jumped in the pickup and roared down to where he was still dancin around. When he saw me comin, he came runnin at me waving his hands over his head hollerin that it was chasin him!! I thought he was havin an LSD hallucination, until I saw a two-foot rattlesnake hooked into the baggy cuff of those britches he wore. The snake had struck at him, but its fangs had hung somehow in those pants and wouldn't come loose!! I had to hold the kid by one arm while I got a shovel out of the truck. The snake was buzzin, the kid was dancin around, and I was trying to chop the snakes head off with the shovel!! After the third try. I finally chopped its head off. That kid went over to a stump and collapsed on it. I cut the rattles off to give to him, but he wouldn't take them. It took him an hour to settle down enough to drive back to Tucson. I bet he hitched his britches up after that!!

Tennis Shoe and Old Jello

Our friend and neighbor, Lyman, needed help gathering a herd of barzona cows off the 90 section DG ranch. It was rough and steep and the canyons were deep and brushy. It was late August and help was nonexistent, so I brought my horses and our two preteen age boys to the works.

Lyman had a full time cowboy and a couple Latin American types who could ride a horse. In those days any Mexican from Mexico could set a horse. The youngest Mexican boy had an unpronounceable name so Lyman just called him Tennis Shoe. He turned out to be a pretty good hand and willing to turn a hand at just about any chore that came along. He could build a rock wall that was as pretty as you could ask for without a speck of mortar. Well, we started this gather. It was hot and, in the afternoons, we got wet from monsoon rains. In what we hoped for a one-week gather was turning into three. Cattle were scattered. There were puddles of water everywhere, so they didn't congregate at the windmills. It was tough. Some days, if we worked 10 sections and got 20 cows, we figured we were doing good.

Now I'm not real high on barzona cows, but in this instance they were sure the right deal. That old ranch had a lot of little flat top mesas on it and those red cows would get right up under the cap rock where no other critter would dare to crawl. Of course, it made it a booger to get to them, steep and shaley, you had to be careful.

One mornin, Lyman ask me to tack a shoe on the horse that Tennis Shoe rode. We all called him Yellow but Tennis Shoe's English was a little sparse, he called that dun pony Jello. Well, when ole Jello lost his shoe, he lost some of his quarter hoof wall so I built a shoe with an extra-long trailer in the heel to cover the broken out spot. When I got through, we struck a trot to the back side of the circle, out beyond a couple of those little steep walled mesas.

Lyman scattered the crew and, as he rode along, was telling me about this one little mesa we were headed for. The walls and slope were steep and covered with Palo Verde, Mesquite, and other noxious brush with big long thorns. Tennis Shoe was the next to last rider who Lyman dropped off. Only I was left as we encircled the mesa. Lyman pointed up high and I could just barely make out a cow's hind quarters behind a tree. That was where I was headed, and it took a little figurin. Big drainages came down off that mesa, many with steep, uncrossable walls. I kept rimmin around, climmin higher and higher, trying to get to where that cow was. The cow tracks became thicker and it was plain there were a lot more cows here than the one we saw. As we climbed and rimmed higher and higher, it became almost impossible for my horse to stand or walk. Finally, I was within a hundred feet or so of where I thought that cow was. I hobbled my horse on a kinda flat place and set off afoot toward where that cow was. When I got to where she shoulda been, there was nothin but deep tracks and thin manure!! And one of those deep tracks was a new horse shoe with an extra-long trailer on it! Down below, I could see a string of red cows winding down a trail with a dun horse following, and a skinny little Mexican kid whoopin it up on him!!

Tom was a Duffass

When we lived in Aguila, we were neighbors with a family who had a big ole piece of country. They ran a few cows and if it rained would stock in feeder steers. The dad was a good ole man. Somewhere in the past he had lost a portion of his one arm, but it didn't slow him down none. He was always busy with some project on the ranch. At the time I met him, he was also battling cancer in his back. He had a son who was fresh married to a pretty good kinda gal, but Tom was an accident waitin to happen. I never met anyone who had as many wrecks as that guy. One evening, he had gone to the corrals to feed the stock. When he didn't come back, long after dark, his wife took a flashlight and went lookin for him. She found him staggering his way home, the side of his head bloody and swole up. Seems he had climbed to the top of the hay stack and was feeding hay into a corral full of cows when he hung the rowels of his spurs in a bale wire and flipped him to the ground, a 25 foot fall! Knocked out, and the side of his head peeled, he had laid there a couple hours with the cattle walkin around on top of him.

Another time, he had asked me to come help them brand some big ole calves that had missed in the works. When I got there, I found they were going to put the calves through a squeeze chute that was made for full grown cows. It wasn't made to adjust to smaller animals but Tom insisted we put them through the chute. I found out later that Tom couldn't throw a rope down a well, let alone catch a cow.

We got started workin and had branded about 20 head when a small black heifer came into the chute. There was no way to hold her. The head gate wouldn't close tight enough and the squeeze wouldn't pinch her either. Tom came to the head gate and ask me to open up, he would grab her and flank her to get her worked. As I eased the gate open, Tom grabbed it, swung it wide open, and ducked into the chute to meet the heifer head on. The heifer was ready. She hit Tom in the chest, bowled him over, and walked the length of him. Tom had wrapped his hands and arms around the heifers neck, on his back, with the heifer buckin and bawlin on top of him. He let go just as I grabbed her by the tail, walked up her side and flanked her. I looked back and Tom was on his hands and knees, head hangin, blood drippin from a tear in his scalp. His wife strolled by with syringes in hand to vaccinate the heifer. She didn't even slow down but did ask if he was ok, not even lookin at him!! His old daddy was brandin the heifer when he looked at me and shook his head. He said Tom had grown up on the ranch but hadn't absorbed enough about it to put in a thimble!!

Asleep at the Switch

Tom was a neighbor; a nice guy but a bumbling boob. He needed help gathering a mountain pasture. Me, my wife, a couple other cowgirls, and Tom's dad went into this mountain pasture to gather a few cows. This pasture was rough, steep, rocky, and cactus strewn. There was a small pond at the base of the main canyon that was spring-fed. This is where the hold-up would be. We left my wife and one of the other gals there to catch everything we threw down to them. The plan was to be out of there by one in the afternoon. It was a five mile drive to the corrals, and that was bad enough.

Myself, Tom's dad, Tom, and a friend of his went up the canyon, two on each side of the stream. Near the summit, the stream channel was un-crossable. Tom and his friend were on one side, Tom's dad and myself were on the other. The agreement was that no one would start down unless we were all together.

We had worked our side of the canyon and was waiting for Tom and his friend, Carl. It was later than we had planned on and needed to get going. No Tom. Soon, Carl came over to the canyon channel and hollered that Tom took off afoot about two hours before and hadn't come back. We drove our cattle down to the girls, then went up Tom's side to meet Carl. He had Tom's horse and said Tom left his horse to go run some cows out of the canyon and hadn't come back. Tom's poor old dad was really worried. We all knew Tom was accident prone and we could imagine him laying somewhere with a broke leg, or worse. The old man and I looked, hollered, and climbed around until almost dark. Finally, the old man said: let's go look down at the pond. We started down and the first person we see is my wife, her Italian temper past boiling.

"THAT LAZY, GOOD-FOR-NOTHING S.O.B. IS ASLEEP UNDER A MESQUITE TREE BELOW THE POND. WHEN I WOKE HIM UP AND TOLD HIM YOU ALL WERE LOOKING FOR HIM SAID: DON'T WORRY, THEY WILL GIVE ME UP FOR DEAD SOON," she said.

Tom didn't know how close to being dead he was!! His dad rimmed his fanny, the other cowgirl chewed his butt because she was supposed to be home hours earlier, and my wife would have cut his throat right there if I had loaned her a knife.

We put 90 head of cows in the corrals by moonlight three hours later. Our kids were home alone, thank god they were responsible kids. Our horses were dinked, and we hadn't had a bite to eat since four that mornin. We swore to never go back, but was softened up by the old man one more time. A few weeks later we went back to help again, but that's another story.

Tom's Big Roundup

Tom had pastured a couple hundred cows for a friend of mine. My friend asked if I would go there and help gather these cows even though I wasn't crazy about workin with Tom. The Mrs. and I went. For three days, we worked this great big pasture, putting our gather in a holding trap every evening. By my count, we were only short about 20 cows when we started work on the fourth day. My wife swore up and down that we had gathered a lot of these cows twice. I wasn't sure of that, but she always had a better memory for individuals than me. Once again, we scattered at the back of a long, rectangular pasture and started working back toward the trap. Once again, we were picking up large bunches of cows. Something was wrong. These cows were getting almost impossible to drive. Instead of west to east, they would run north to south. I had left Mrs. jefe on the south edge of the drive on a damn good mount so I knew there wouldn't be a screw up.

About half way through the drive, I saw a pickup boiling toward me from the south. A fellow was in the back waving at me and yelling. Damn hunters, I thought. When they got there, they told me the Mrs. had had a wreck and was hurt. It was two miles down to where she was, so I tied my horse and rode down to where she was with the hunters. Her horse was tied close and the horn and forks of her saddle were packed in dirt and greasewood. She was sitting, propped up against a mesquite tree, in the shade, obviously in great pain. She had been trying to turn a goofy ole cow and hadn't seen a low mesquite tree. Her horse had seen it and tried to jump it, hanging his front feet in the top of the little tree. This caused a cartwheel with the Mrs. underneath the wheel!! We loaded her in the truck, drove to our truck, change rides, and I headed to the hospital 30 miles away.

While there, the hunters gathered up my horses and took them to the corrals for us. I never even got their names or saw them again. Not all hunters are stinkers.

At the hospital, we found out she had a broken collar bone. A wrap, a sling, and some pain pills and we headed home. That night was a booger. The kids didn't like my cookin, the Mrs. couldn't get comfortable, every move hurt. All the while, she kept telling me that the cow she was driving at the time of the wreck was a cow she had gathered two times before.

Tom came to the house and said we had all the cows gathered and we would ship the next morning. The Mrs. assured me she would be ok, for me to go and quit fussin over her.

The next mornin, five of us set about gathering the trap as the trucks were to be there at noon. There were lots of tracks of the cattle, but, the farther we rode, it was evident there wasn't any cattle in the trap! Soon, I heard a yell over to my right so I loped over there. One of the other riders was sitting on his horse looking at about a hundred yards of laid-over fence with a trail a foot-deep and a yard-wide goin over it!! Tom rode up and looked at it and, in a whipped voice, explained the fence had been up the last time he checked it. His dad asked when that was. Last year, he whimpered.

Tom looked at his 75 year old dad, with one arm and a cancer growin in his back and ask him to go get some posts and fix the fence!! The rest of us turned our horses and headed back to the trailers. I heard Tom's dad say, in a firm voice, for Tom to fix the fence or he would call off the trucks and call the cows owners. I don't know what would have been worse, makin excuses for a pitiful excuse of a son or fixin the fence.

Ropin

Stepped on My Eyes

1970, Mormon Lake ropin, 4th of July. I'm batchin out of the bed of my pickup, got coffee on the Colman stove, horses fed, cookin breakfast. My friend, who is a Babbit cowpuncher, is still asleep in his teepee. But, with the smell of the coffee, he crawls out on his hands and knees. When I hand him the coffee, he looks up with two black eyes!! Knowing there had been a wild dance at the lodge the night before, I ask the question and he replied, someone stepped on my eyes!!!

I Run Real Fast

My friend, Dean, had just got married. I had just got divorced. We were all at a cookout and ropin/playday. Just a good time Saturday afternoon among friends and classmates. One of the events was ribbon roping. For those who don't know how it works, a ribbon is rubber banded to a calf's tail. The roper catches the calf, and a girl runner pulls the ribbon and runs to the finish line, fastest time wins. Dean's new wife came to me and asked if I would rope a calf for her. I paid the entry fee and we entered. When our turn came, I roped the calf quick was half way down the rope when this blonde streak went by with the ribbon in hand! We won hands down. Turned out, she was a sprinter for the ASU women's track team!!!! Ringer all the folks yelled as we counted the winnings!!! When she asked me to rope she simply said, I run real fast. Then, when she picked up the winnins, they give her a little bitty first place ribbon with about 200 dollars in cash. She brought it back and said all she wanted was the ribbon!!! I think Dean choked on his beer!!!

Empty Stash

In the early70s thru the 80s, rodeo producer/promoter Bill Roer produced what he called the rope a thon. Eight days of ropin at his place in Laveen. The arena seemed like it was a quarter mile long with a 25 foot score. Big, hard-runnin steers made it a challenge. One of the most popular ropins was the feedlot event. Only feedlot employees or owners could rope. In those days, there were plenty of feedlots and cowboys who roped. Dude was a friend of mine who

worked at the same feedlot as I did. His wife was a moderating factor
in his life, or he would have been like the rest of us: harum-scarum
with our money. Dude had been savin his shekels for months so he
could go to Roer's. On the day the entries were due, he went home
to get his cash. When he went to check his stash, he found it empty.
Going to his wife with the empty sock, she merely pointed to the
laundry room at a new washer and drier. That's yours and Roer's, she
said!!! Dude didn't get to go that year!!

Partner Joe and I

Partner Joe and I worked together at a couple feed yards. We also
roped together at the feedlot ropins and open events. We had been
on a good three year roll placing about everywhere and winnin a few.
We didn't know it at the time, but people were callin us those feedlot
assholes! We seemed to have a habit of comin from behind to place.
We were at a feedlot ropin in Maricopa when it got down to the short
go. I had legged our first steer and didn't think we would get a call in
the short. I had pulled the wood off my pony when Joe loped up and
hollered we would get a run!! I re-saddled and loped my cold horse
back to the arena. Joe was already in the header's box when I got
there. When in the heeler's box, I looked at Joe and he was grinnin
at me. I had seen that before and knew what it meant. He nodded
and threw 30 foot of rope 32 feet and ducked. One blind swing at the
corner and the clock stopped at 5!! It was there the announcer (along
with a lot whiskey) called us assholes!!! We split second and third!!!

Old-Time Rodeo Hand

Years ago, when I was an aspiring team roper, there was an
old-time rodeo hand in Casa Grande who owned a bar. There was
another roper there who shall remain nameless (he is still with us)
who bet the old timer he could rope 10 muley steers without a time
limit, without a miss. The time was set and lots of side bets were
made. The original bet was a lot of money for the day and time. The
night of the event, the whole team roping community turned out to
watch. The old hand climbed up on the fence to watch and heckle the
roper. There was no time limit set, so when the first steer was turned

out, the roper casually loped the steer to the bottom of the arena then followed the steer around until he began to trot. At that point, he stood up in his stirrups, took dead aim, swang three times and MISSED!!! A collective groan went up from the crowd! We all decided drinkin beer would be more interesting that night!!!

Get Ready, Big Boy

Years ago, when we lived in a town with a real great ropin club, Mrs. jefe was in the lead for a series ropin saddle. We were right down to the end and the points were close between Mrs. jefe and a good friend who was local businessman. When the ropin started, Herb and Mrs. jefe were partnered up about equal. Thank god el jefe was only ropin with one of them!! When it came to the short round, only 2/10 of a second separated the two. Herb was to go first and he and his partner made a good solid run. when he came back he said, "If I let a woman beat me tonight, I'll quit ropin!" As Mrs. jefe rode by on her way to the box, she said without lookin right or left, "Well, get ready, big boy. You're about to sell out." Herb didn't win the saddle, but he didn't sell out either!!!

Paint Mare

Years ago, we rented the property where George Aro's arena is now. We there to receive and care for Mexican steers that were being pastured on three different ranches in Pinal County. We didn't have any help, just me, Mrs., and three teenage kids. The steers came every night from Nogales, Douglas and Sasabee. We didn't get a lot of sleep.

One afternoon when I had 15 minutes I wasn't needed somewhere, I was tryin to tack a shoe on a pony who wasn't a lot of fun to shoe. It was during the big Indian Rodeo in Casa Grande when a truck and trailer pulled into the yard. An Indian fellow got out and introduced himself and told me so and so. Told him I rode colts and trained rope horses. Well, I knew this Indian fellow by reputation and, while he was a great silversmith, he had a bad habit of not payin what he owed.

I told this gentleman I didn't have time to ride his horse, but thank you anyway. He wouldn't take no for an answer and he wouldn't leave. I told him that I charged twice what anyone else charged. That didn't make any difference. I was under this horse's hind leg when he kept on about how I ought to ride this horse for him. I pointed to an empty corral with my hammer and said around a mouthful of nails, put her there if you miss one payment I'll keep your horse. I put my head down, nailin on the shoe. Pretty soon, I heard his truck start and drive away.

In the corral, he left a four year old black and white paint mare. And I NEVER saw that gentleman again. And that mare made a whumpus kitty rope horse that I rode to many a set of heels in the junior rodeo circuit. When I finally sold her, she still kept on giving because she kept Carter in school another semester.

Prescott, Prescott

Pete and I were havin a beer on the front porch of Pete's house. His new wife was inside cookin supper with her mother. Pete and I were discussin goin to Prescott to the rodeo. Pete's mother-in-law stuck her head out the door, PRESCOTT, PRESCOTT that's all I hear you ought to have prescott up yore ass!! Pete never looked at her, took a sip of beer and said ain't room with all the other stuff you told me to stick up there!!

The Old Timer

The old timer worked at Tovreas with the rest of us idiots. What a hand. His horses were always the best handlin and he knew the right place to be all the time. He taught me a lot, some good some bad, cause ya see, he was a bad drinker, gambler, womanizer, and just all-around rounder. Once, at a ropin in Tucson (a bar called the Buckskin that had an arena out the backdoor), he matched us in a five steer ropin. The other team was damn good at match ropins, but when it was over we had won by a tenth of a second. I was loadin the horses while he collected the winnins. When he came back, he handed me a pile of cash!! I ask how much we won, a thousand a man he said!! But I didn't have a thousand to gamble I said!! I didn't either, he said but they didn't know that when I matched em!!! We got outta town and stayed for a while!!!

Feed Yard Ropins

A little history on feed yard ropins. The first three or four were produced by Pfizer Pharmaceuticals, who was a real popular outfit for vaccines, antibiotics, and such. This was in the mid-1960s, and they were held at Frank Powels arena at 32nd street and Southern in Phoenix. This was a real popular place to rope in those days. A free barbeque was available and the winners got a ton of feed supplement, as well as gold buckles. This was in the days when buckles were rare and saddles were unheard of. As I remember, there were like 50 teams at the first one, and from then on it grew. I remember lots of people trying to get weekend jobs in feed yards so they could qualify to enter. Only feed yard employees could enter and you had to show proof when you entered, a pay stub. Usually, a PRCA member was drafted to flag and Frank Powel furnished the cattle. These were muley cattle and the ropin was tie down. Dally ropin was unheard of at that time. only those lily white Californians did that!!

I can remember winners from those ropins, but not which ones, you see the Tovreas crew won the first four ropins held. Sam White, Pete Black, Gilbert Flores, A.D. Browning, Buster Hall, all had Pfizer buckles. I didn't get one because the first few years I was the kid and someone had the duty of watchin the yard at home. But as time went on and other people produced feed yard ropins, I got my chance. As my old friend, Weldon Rutledge, would say, there will always be another ropin and we will all be there!

Bill Roer produced a feed yard ropin during his ropeathon in Laveen. Producers Cattle Feeders produced one, as did AZL in Queen Creek at the Hughes and Ganz feed yard. By then, it had transformed into a dally ropin.

And, then, CALF magazine got into the act. They formed the International Feed Yard Roping Association. They cut the U.S. into regions and Canada with qualifying ropins in each region. The first five teams in each category was eligible to go to the finals, with the first one held in Las Vegas, and then they were held indoors in Elko, Nevada, after that. After the third one in Elko, I quit workin feed yards and was not eligible to compete, but that's how it started, it was a lot of fun. There were a lot of good hands in them days both in the arena and at the feed yard. To name a few, Bill Magill, Johnny

Rodriguez Mike Benitas, Pablo Osuna, John Clem, and my old friend and partner, Joe Clem. Most are gone now but not forgotten.

George Mason

I just got word my old friend, George Mason, who was a stock contractor, brand inspector, and WWII hero has passed. He had to be in his 90s. We will all miss him. Years ago, when I was a kid and George was contractin rodeos, he had an old sorrel horse in his bareback string that was a real treat to watch. They always ran him in last during the performance. He would generally buck off his rider or when the rider got off, then ole sorrely would run to the pickup man and stop, stand stock still while they unsaddled him in the arena, they would then saddle him with a ropin saddle and run the first steer in the team roping!!! A better tie down horse it was hard to find!!! You would never know unless you were watchin the bareback ridin it was the same horse!!

Hawkeye

Years ago, I left Maricopa at 3 in the mornin headed to Mormon Lake for the ropins there on the 4th of July. I left early because I was traveling by myself and wanted to be there in time for the first ropin. At Cordes Junction there used to be an all-night cafe called the Hub. Well when I got there I decided I was ahead of schedule so I stopped for breakfast. As I pulled into the parking lot I could see a big bonfire down at the end with a lot of motorcycles parked around. There were Hell's Angel types walking around the cafe and down at the bonfire. There were two highway patrol cars parked side by side watching the party. I eased up as close to those guys as I could and parked, figuring they would keep the bikers away from my stuff while I ate.

I unloaded my horse and tied him to the back of the trailer and as I walked to the cafe one of the patrolmen told me not to worry about my outfit. When I got inside there were two bikers holding a third between them at the cash register making him pay his bill. One apologized to the waitress and said their rude friend wouldn't be back. An old friend who lived nearby was there having breakfast, so we sat together, visited, and ate.

When I got back outside there was no patrolmen in sight and 2 bikers were sittin on the hood of my truck. Seeing no other way around I walked on by, loaded my horse and walked up to the cab. As I walked by the truck I glanced in the back and my bedroll and camp outfit seemed all there. As I got to the cab the bikers slid down to the ground and walked away, one looked back and said, "Your outfit is all there. Hawkeye said to watch it." Before I could ask who Hawkeye was, they were gone. I went on to Mormon Lake, roped for three days, made a little money, and had a good time.

Back at home, it was work as usual. Same ole feedlot grind. About a month later, I was sick of my own cookin and decided to go to Maricopa to the Headquarters Cafe for supper, and to the bar next door afterwards. As I walked into the cafe there was a schoolmate of mine that I played football with sittin there eating supper also. I slid into the booth with him and we visited while he ate. He was a few years older than me but was always a friend. He was just getting through when my supper showed up and I offered to buy him a drink when I got done but he said his ole lady was on the way to pick him up. Just then, a real attractive, long-legged blonde in biker leather walked up and asked, "Hawkeye are you ready to go?" Then, I knew who Hawkeye was.

Fire!!

Years ago, if you were a rodeo hand in Arizona, during the Fourth of July weekend you went two places: Prescott or Mormon Lake. If you were real dedicated you made both. Mormon Lake, outside Flagstaff, had a steak house lodge with a bar, a ropin arena, a few private cabins, and lots of camping space in the pines. For three or four days, daylight to dark, they had a ropin goin on. In Prescott it was the world's oldest rodeo goin on. A great show, street dances on Whiskey Row, and all kinds of different events. A lot of team ropers would enter Prescott, rope their steer, load up, and run the hour and a half to Mormon Lake. 500 teams was unheard of at most places but Mormon Lake. Rufus Brown always furnished the steers. Big, tough, hard-runnin steers that most ropers today would whine about, but we were so damn dumb we didn't know any better.

With so many ropers there and everybody camping out, it got kinda crowded. So crowded that if you needed to leave it was almost impossible. You might have to get three or four people to break camp and move their rigs just so you could get to the road!!

In them days, motorhomes were unheard of and living quarter trailers were rare. Most of us had a six pack camper on a pickup with a two-horse trailer!! Maybe a canvas fly off one side for a little shade. Partner Joe and I had rigged our outfits so we could stretch a tarp between the two campers, real homey. We had a little camp table and kept a poker game goin between go rounds. There were loud speakers strung in the trees all through camp. So you kept an ear cocked for a team number that was close to yours and then you had time to get ready!! Some of those poker games got almost as rich as the ropins!! Joe would sit back and braid headstalls and bridle reins to sell for entry fees and poker money. If you won somethin that day, you went to the steakhouse and ate that night, then some dancin, and a few drinks. If not, you kicked back in camp, drank your own beer and cooked a burger, BSin' with your neighbor. Good times!!

One year, right in the middle of the Saturday ropin, someone hollered fire!! We all looked up and the lodge was smokin, flames lickin out the second story windows!! There was no fire department in 30 miles and, if there was, it couldn't get to the lodge anyway for all the trucks. The ropin announcer said that any one not ropin needed to take their family and horses and climb the hill behind the arena to safety!! The ropin went on. The forest service showed up with some hotshots and were tryin to contain all they could. That hillside wasn't real safe, lots of big pine trees, dry as all get out and that lodge was puttin out lots of sparks!! There was no way to get your trucks out. Talk about gridlock!! Some brave soul was runnin water from a garden hose on the 1000 gallon propane tank right next to the lodge, flames lickin the tank as he worked at keepin it cool. Pretty soon, the forest service people told us to move back more because a slurry bomber was gonna make a drop on the lodge. A lead plane passed over, then the bomber splattered the lodge with pink slurry, not to mention every truck, trailer, and unattended horse or roper!! But the fire was out, and the ropin never stopped. Just goes to show you the dedication of team ropers!!

July Fourth

I spent the mornin trying to come up with a cowboy story that would fit in with today. I remember a lot of the Independence Days I spent at ropins, rodeos, and such. A few I spent at home or workin, but I can't remember a one that I wasn't proud to be an American cowboy. The story I'll tell you today will show the great length that cowboys go through to celebrate the Fourth. And, in this case, I had an added incentive as you'll see.

For six years, I was a member of the Arizona National Guard. This one year, some fool scheduled our summer camp at Fort Irwin outside of Barstow, California, over the Fourth of July weekend!! I had partners at Mormon Lake who was countin on me to be there!! (Not to mention me countin on being there!) When I left on the convoy to Barstow, I entrusted my truck, trailer, and horse to a cute brunette I was datin. I had no idea how we would do it, but I told her we were goin to Mormon Lake the next weekend!!

Thursday afternoon, I had found a ride to Phoenix from Barstow. I called my dolly and told her to have the truck packed, gassed, and ole Rabbit in the trailer Friday afternoon and we would hit the trail to Flagstaff. If all worked out, we would be at Mormon Lake Saturday mornin for the first ropin.

Sure enough, I landed at dolly's door step about 4 p.m. Friday, stepped out of one crowded car into that ford rodeo rig and we scorched the road to Mormon Lake. And, sure enough, we were ropin Saturday. Didn't win a dime. Partied and danced then got a good night's sleep in preparation for Sunday's ropin. Roped Sunday mornin, blew out in the first round, loaded up, headed back to Phoenix to catch my ride back to Barstow. Six of us packed in a car, headed back. Driver got tired let some other cannon cocker drive. We all went to sleep, and a while later the driver woke us to tell us he was lost!!! We were in San Bernardino!!! Fool missed Barstow!!! We were gonna be AWOL!!! Got turned around, drove like hell back the way we came, rolled into the barracks, ran through, changing clothes, out the back door into formation just in time to hear our names called in roll.

All that and it was worth every minute of the trip!! Dolly took care of ole Rabbit, the Ford, and when I got back from summer camp, made a lifelong commitment to go down the road with me!!! She's still here and why I don't know, but every fourth I think of that trip. It's hell to get old, but this country just gets better and better with each birthday. Yeah, we got problems, but nothin can't be fixed. Where else on Earth can a young man and woman do what we did?

The All-Girl Ropin

Years ago, the girl rodeo contestants needed to raise some money for a worthy cause of some sort, I don't remember what. Since I was a certified judge/flagman for their barrel races, I was invited to judge this event. Never could turn down a smilin blonde. This event was held at Frank Powell's arena at 36th and Southern in Phoenix. Frank furnished the cattle for all kinds of fun events. A calf dressing event, where a three girl team roped and put a pair of bloomers on a calf; an all-girl roping; a ribbon roping, where a male roper would rope a calf and the lady would pull a ribbon off the tail of the calf and race back to the finish line. Lots of fun. Lots of beer consumed. Which led us to the last event: a Jeep ropin. A local car dealer had donated the use of a brand new Jeep for the use of this event. The Jeep was backed into the header's box. A driver, a roper, and two girls in the back loaded up. a calf turned out, the driver roarin up to the calf, the roper catchin the calf and tyin the rope to the roll bar a la John Wayne in Hatari!! The girls jump out and tie the calf to get a time. Great fun!! Now this Jeep was yellow, chrome bumper, and tuck and roll upholstery, fancy, powered by a 283 Chevy engine. This thing was as hot as it looked!!!

All went well until Gene Ray, Tommy, and their two gals were up. Now Gene and Tommy were two of the best ropers anywhere, bar none. But they were also chanpeen beer drinkers!! When the gate was opened, Gene Ray was drivin and started runnin that yellow Jeep through the gears. Tommy was standin up to the roll bar swingin his twine in anticipation of a quick catch. The girls in the back cheerin them on!! The calf wasn't goin for this deal at all and made bee line for the left fence, then made a sharp right and headed down the arena for home. When Gene got to the left fence, he forgot to make that right hand turn!! The Jeep hit a light pole, dead center, in third gear. Tommy flew over the roll bar and made contact with the same light pole!! The two girls in the back slammed into the seats!! That stopped the cheering. Two bloody noses, Tommy out cold, and Gene Ray walked away untouched, lookin for a beer!!! That pretty little Jeep had a permanent crease right dead center all the way back to the driver's seat!! I don't know who, if anyone, paid for that Jeep, but I heard later that car dealer almost lost his religion over that deal!!

Mike

Mike could rope. I haven't seen him in years. I'll bet he can still rope, if he is alive. Ya see, Mike didn't just sip at life, he ran against it with a funnel in his mouth. He was a good hand with horses, a damn good cowboy, and a hell of a horse shoer. But he was doin his best to run out his string, as fast as he could. A lot of people didn't like Mike, but he and I got along well. We traveled together, roped together, partied together, but he sure could stir the pot. Once, on our way home from a ropin, we stopped at a Circle K for a little octane (for us, not the truck). As we were walkin across the parkin lot, a song that was popular about then was playin on the sound system outside the store. Ray Stevens, "The Streak." Well, Mike just kinda did a shuffle and sashayed around an old lady on the way to her car. She kinda bristled up and says "what is this." Mike says this is a streak... and started peelin his clothes!! I went in for the beer while he put his clothes back on, as we drove off a cop was pullin in to the K. Nobody ever said anything, but I had to keep an eye on Mike for a while.

Mike was prone to disappear once in a while, for months at a time, but he was a good enough hand that when he did show up he would get hired on no problem. We were practicin one evening in May when his header missed a steer. Mike spurred up and, using the fence for a hazer, got down on the steer. Now ANYBODY who bulldogs knows not to do that. Well, sure enough Mike houlihaned the steer and broke his leg, Mike's not the steer. When the doc got through, Mike had a cast from ankle to crotch. It was a month and a half until the Fourth of July. Doc told him not to plan on goin. Well, you guessed it, he went, cut the cast off, and would freeze the leg before he roped. Won a wagon load of money. A month later, he seemed just fine except for the little hop he had when he walked, but he said that was OK, the girls all thought it was sexy!!!

Rodeos and Ropins

Some of my earliest memories of rodeos and ropins were of the old Phoenix jaycee rodeo held at the fairgrounds in Phoenix. I couldn't have been more than five or six when my Dad took me there the first time. The old concrete stadium was packed, as it was every time after that we went. My Dad was a fan of rodeo. He knew all the contestants and what they competed in, where they came from, and who was world champions. I never realized he kept track of that stuff since he didn't compete. He could rope, and rope well, but just never competed. Some of the best times I had as a kid was getting to go to the rodeos with him.

When the fair commission built the coliseum at the fairgrounds, we went to a lot of rodeos and ropin events. I remember watchin Dale Smith and Bill Hamilton in a match calf ropin there, ten head for a 1000 dollars a side. Big money in those days. I think Hamilton won. As a few years past, I remember competing in team ropings at that building. It was a little tight for tie-down ropings, but you could dally rope there without too much trouble. At that time, that old barn was the only indoor facility in Arizona. I showed horses there, roped there, and watched a lot of great rodeo contestants there.

As the years past, the jaycee rodeo fell to the wayside. Why, I never really knew. I miss it to this day. Another rodeo that has drifted away was the Chandler Sheriff's Posse rodeo. A great outdoor rodeo. I remember watching the bucking horse war paint there and, yes, he got his man.

One night, I was at a roping at Frank Powell's arena at 36th and Southern. I was a bit cocky as I had been on a good roll and a couple pretty girls were followin me around to the ropins I went to. Frank come over to me and asked if I had all my partners as there was a guy there who needed a header. He was the world champion bull rider. I said, "So what, can he rope?" I didn't rope with that bull rider world champion, but the guys that did won the ropin with him. Now, that was a weekend punkin roller but it was as important to Larry Mahan as winning the world as a bull rider!! Go figure, what kind of dummy am I?

As the years went by, I was able to compete at some great venues, indoors and out. I was able to meet and socialize with world champions and also rans. One of the most classy gentlemen I ever met was world champion team roper John Miller. A pure gentleman and always the same to everyone whether you were a beginner or a pro. He was well mounted at all times and treated his horses as athletes and partners who he gave credit for his success. I got to know John a little better in later years as we were goin to junior rodeos at the same time with our kids. One of his friends was Ace Berry. Ace went to the NFR numerous times as a bareback rider AND a heeler for John. Now there aren't many contestants who were able to do that!! And he was a class act too. Both those fellers was raised by the movie actor and team roper world champion Ben Johnson. But for all Ben wanted to help him, John did it on his own. John's kids are still ropin today, I believe, and I haven't seen john in a long time, but I'll bet you he's still the class act he was then.

One of the earliest memories of rodeo was being at the Phoenix rodeo and watching Ben Johnson rope. We were sitting up pretty high in the stands, but to this day I remember that rope making a cracking sound when Ben roped those horns!! Then there was Wilber Plaugher who clowned and fought bulls. When the bull doggin came around, Wilber crawled on a horse in his clown get up and dogged a steer, not as a gag, he was competing, and I believe he got a check almost everywhere he went. Well, there it is. It's been a great ride, and I met some great folks, and I hope to meet more!!

Footrace

In the early days of civilization, footracing was a popular entertainment. It made a short resurgence in the early 70s around the rodeo and jackpot roping community. The big gun was Ray. He was fresh back from Vietnam, had a little money, and liked to gamble. Before I met Ray, he had already outran the backfield of the ASU football team and was working on any other suckers who would step up with cash in hand. As time went on and ray outran more people, it became harder and harder to get a match. So, he started giving up distance at the start. His favorite race was the length of a roping arena, giving the opposition a head start of one third the arena, then with Ray in the catch pen, the race was started. Ray had to jump the fence into the arena, then go catch his opposition. A few of those races were close, real close, but I never knew him to loose.

At Mormon Lake Fourth of July ropin, Ray was ropin and tryin to get a match up, no takers. He gave up half the arena, no takers. He offered to smoke a pack of cigarettes and drink a six pack of beer before the race, no takers. Finally, in desperation, he offered to match his new wife against any other woman there and, when he couldn't get a match on that, offered to match his six month old boy against any other kid the same age at crawlin!! Never got a one.

The last race I saw Ray run he about did himself in. We were at the old 35th and Baseline Arena when somehow he matched Bill Roer a race. Now Bill was 60 plus and Ray was in his mid-30s. Bill was a hell of an athlete for his age and loved to gamble. The terms were: Ray started in the catch pen laying on his belly; Bill got two thirds the arena start, but had to run backwards. This was for a thousand a man. At the drop of the flag, Bill was off trottin backwards watchin Ray jump the fence flat-footed then come on like a house afire! Bill was nearing the finish line and those of us who bet against him could see our money flying away. It seemed there was no way Ray would make up the distance. That old man was running backwards as fast as some people ran forwards!! Just as Bill was in reach of the finish line, he fell! It knocked the wind out of him and he was laying on his back wheezing for air as Ray ran by. Now, all Bill had to do was reach back and put his hand over the finish line to win, but he told me later he wasn't sure where he was. As far as I know, there wasn't any footraces after that one, but Ray said he would never gamble with Bill Roer again

Match Ropins

At one time, match ropins were a popular event. I'll bet x amount I can out rope ya! I've seen as many as three or four teams get a match up for as little as 50 a man, then winner take all. It takes a whole different mindset to do that kind of ropin. At a rodeo you rope each go round as fast as you can. At a jackpot you try to rope all your cattle and win the average. A match ropin, you just rope a little better than the other guy, but not the absolute best you can. You got to pay attention to what the other team is doin, what your doin, and know the cattle by their first names!! There has been a lot of match ropins in the calf roping world, still a popular deal in states where they rope lots of calves. Team ropin matches have kinda fallin out of favour in Arizona. I don't really know why, could be a lot of reasons.

The first match ropin I competed in was in Tucson. My partner was an old gambler, roper, pool player, and down ride scoundrel, but he knew how to match rope. We won the match and if I would have known what we were ropin for, I might have choked, but AD didn't tell me. But what he did on each steer was tell me what the steer was, and where to rope him and how to handle him. We won by just a few tenths of a second, but we could have won by more. But, we didn't show them all we had. Kinda like hustlin pool. We matched those boys a couple more times before they give up. If we had shown every card we had, all we would have got was the first match. Plus, no one else would have matched us. I didn't know all this at the time we did this, but learned as we went along.

Years later, we belonged to a ropin club and some of the members thought it would be neat if we had a match ropin after the Saturday night ropin. After about six weeks of this, those same fellers was wanting to ban the matches. Seems I had a partner who was a pretty slick header and could get the rope out of his hand pretty quick, but he didn't think about what was down the road. The last match we had was a two-header. There were four teams entered. I don't remember the amount we roped for, wasn't a lot, 25 a man maybe. I had, at the time, a little blue roan heel horse who was as quick as I ever rode with a sudden stop. Judd turned our first steer just across the line and the clock stopped at 5 flat. The other teams were in the 7 seven second range, so I knew we had a lot of leeway, but Judd didn't see it that way. Second steer he turned even quicker. I tracked the steer four jumps and roped him by two feet. 6 flat!! At that time, that was an arena record for that arena on two steers. The rest of the teams went long and we beat them by a big margin. By the next ropin, they had banned matches. Don't get me wrong, I lost a lot of match ropins, probably as many as I won, but I never complained about someone ropin better than me. I just went home and practiced harder or tried to make my horse better. Not so today, everyone is handicapped, so those who don't want to work as hard as someone else still has a chance to win his money back. I hate whiners and those with weak hearts.

Jingle Bells

When I was in high school, I got the horse show bug. Of courses, we all know that high school age boys haven't a bit of common sense. I was no exception. I had bred a mare to an Appaloosa stud and gotten a wild-colored, blanket-hipped horse colt. By the time I was a sophomore in high school, I had that horses broke to do just about everything you could think of. Naturally, you could rope off him. He wasn't a bad western pleasure horse. Trail courses were a piece of cake and reining was just boring. We won every 4-H class there was available, so we moved on to the breed shows. We were placing very place we went and winning some. One of my fellow competitors made a wise crack about the only thing we didn't do was a costume class. In the Appaloosa world, this entailed dressing up like an Indian and riding around the ring showing off how well-broke your horses was and how authentic your costume was.

I said something to my mom and she got started. I went to the library (weren't no internet then) and got a book on the Nez Perce Indian tribes, the people who raised the Appaloosa horses before the white man contaminated the breed with draft horses. Well, I found out that the Nez Perce tribe was fond of bells on their clothes, their horses, and anything they could tie them to. So I bought a BIG string of big ole jingle bells and had mom sew them all over the costume. Then, before the class entered the ring, I braided a bunch more in my horse's mane and tail.

Since I never had shown in a costume class before I had paid attention to a couple classes at previous shows. A wise old trainer who took a liking to me told me always be the first in the ring or the last, the judge looks at those the hardest. Well, I hung back in the shadows when the costume class was to enter the ring. When everyone was in and I was the last to enter, I stirred ole App up into a dead run and came into the ring with all those bells a jinglin like Santa Clause on Christmas Eve. I had a war bridle on my pony and feathers damn near draggin the ground. As I passed each other horse in the ring I heard the crowd roar. I figured they were just impressed at my great, authentic costume. As I lapped the arena I noticed no one else was horse back. Some were trying to catch their horses who had run to the far end of the arena. The crowd was laughing so hard you couldn't hear the loud speaker.

Casey Darnel was the judge and he was standing in the middle of the ring crooking his finger at me. I slowed down to a trot and rode over to him.

"Just wait here kid," he told me. "Let those other folks catch their horses so I can figure out who wins second and third." Thus ended my costume class career. By the next year I had outgrown my costume and the desire to compete in that class. Besides, if I told someone I was gonna enter, no one else would!!

www.ingramcontent.com/pod-product-compliance
Lightning Source LLC
Chambersburg PA
CBHW021546290526
45785CB00004BA/1589